NOVEMBER BELOW HEART MOUNTAIN:
A Hunting Story

Ben Walters

_____

NOVEMBER BELOW HEART MOUNTAIN:
A Hunting Story

FRONT COVER PHOTO: Heart Mountain, 2005 photo
by my dad. BACK COVER PHOTO: I took this looking
down into Buckhorn Basin where I shot the easy
cow.

Chapter 15 is called The Torch, Part 2, and is an
adapted version of my story published by the Rocky
Mountain Elk Foundation's *Bugle* magazine.

ISBN-10: 0692223479
ISBN-13: 978-0-692-22347-5

Preface

I WAS ASKED THE OTHER DAY WHAT is the first thing I remember in my life, an easy question because my first memory in this life is about a gun. I can clearly recall my mom picking me up from pre-school at age four and taking me to the Boy Scout store to get a Daisy Model 299 Boy Scout BB gun. I still have that gun. My next memories are about begging my dad almost every night to open his gun cabinet and let me look at his rifles and shotguns and pistols. Then after that it was about doing everything I could to find toy reproductions of those rifles and hunt all "season" long in the back yard or down at the park, packs of crayons serving as extra cartridges. In the ninth grade, prior to my building my own gun cabinet, I went over to my best friend's house after school one day to look at his dad's rifles. I nearly fainted when I saw how many they had — stored in a walk-in safe. That firmly established my need to build and fill my own modest cabinet with a selection of rifles, the latter of which seems to take an unfairly long time. My mom says I had at least one of every type of toy gun ever sold. My wife now tries to convince me that I do not need to have at least one of every type of real gun ever sold. Clearly these early memories have had some sort of powerful influence on my actions.

Although this isn't a gun story, when you remove your rifle from its case, somewhere in the stillness of the prairie or the mountains in the pre-dawn chill and darkness, it's like lining up for kickoff in a football game. Here is where it gets real. So hunting, in my world, begins with a high-powered rifle, but it's so much more than that. This is a story I've been dreaming, planning, and acting out for nearly forty years now, in Idaho and in Montana, and in all kinds of different weather and across sagebrush foothills, timbered hillsides, and steep rocky slopes.

I haven't always been successful at hunting, where success is defined as making a clean kill, but I think I may have achieved the paramount of personal accomplishment in this endeavor. I have carved out a blueprint of what hunting means to me, and I have learned to live it. I do not define a good hunt anymore based on the numbers of game animals I see or the blood I spill, but rather as a feeling I get before, during, and after any hunt. It's tough to describe this feeling, but I'm going to try. The hunts related in this book almost always end in harvesting the animal, not because that's what I consider a perfect hunt, but because it would get boring reading about going home empty-handed all the time. Not boring to do, just boring to read about.

Introduction - The Bull

THEY CALL IT "BUCK FEVER," but in this case you'd call it "bull fever" because there was a bull elk standing there and I was supposed to be shaking like a leaf. But there was none of that now. I had promised myself that morning that I was not going to miss, no matter what. I had promised myself that I would get my shot today. I just knew that today was that day. I had prepared for this moment for 30 years, and I was not going to blow it. This was my first, most legitimate, and best chance I'd ever had at taking one of these big bastards. Evidently the elk was going to cooperate as well; he just stood there broadside, 400 yards away, and watched me throw my backpack into the snow in front of me, watched me flop down prone, and watched me level my .338 Winchester Magnum at him. Every other elk I'd ever encountered would have been at least in the next drainage by then. Maybe there is more chance and luck to hunting than I'd previously thought. Why wasn't this bull bugging out?

I caught a last glance of Heart Mountain through those diamond ice crystals that form in the air on frigid mornings. There was a curl of snow blowing off it as I shimmied on my elbows through the snow mattress and into position. Perfect rest: rifle across the ditched backpack, my left hand settled over the forestock just in front of the scope, and right hand on the black grip of the rifle stock, trigger finger inside the trigger guard because it's game time, and my thumb clicking the safety into the vertical "fire position."

At this point, if you had a case of buck fever, your scope's crosshairs would be moving in figure-eight patterns around your target as you tried in vain to control your breathing and your heart rate. You'd want it to be just like practice at the range, but it wouldn't be. The only similarity between that and this would be the rifle. You wouldn't squeeze the trigger like you were taught; you'd slap or pull that thing like you were trying to separate it from the rifle.

I didn't have any of that right now. My crosshairs glued immediately to that area just behind the front shoulder, which we called the "firebox" because behind it are the heart and lungs and a quick and humane death. I squeezed that modified trigger to the crisp point of contact and CRACK! the shot was off. Then it's kind of like teeing off at the golf course; you're not supposed to raise your head and admire your work. You're supposed to stay focused on that target as best you can for that post-shot split-second follow-through.

On cold mornings, a rifle report gets eaten up pretty quickly across an open flat. It seems more like a sharp clap, but it's definitely out of place in such a silent setting. Then, if you made a good shot, you can usually hear another slap or thud when the sound of the bullet making contact with the animal returns to you. There was no slap or thud now. In fact, after the quick crack of the rifle, everything returned to exactly as it had been before. The bull was still just looking at me. So on instinct, I worked the bolt on my Weatherby and put round number two in the chamber. Same glued crosshairs, same squeeze, same rifle report, same result. This time, though, the bull had had enough and the big rack turned to the left and he started galloping the hell out of there. And then here came the bull fever; I was wondering when I would lose it. Including the shell in the chamber, a Weatherby Vanguard Series 2 rifle, .338 Winchester Magnum, has four rounds. Two had been spent and the other two left that rifle as if it were fully automatic and not a bolt action. BANGBANG. I suppose anyone within earshot that morning probably heard only three total shots, because only the first two had any time-space between them. It would have sounded like BANG-BANG-BBANG. And the elk crossed over the top into Elk Creek looking perfectly healthy. The last thing I saw was that rack cresting the ridge.

1—Sighting In

POW! SILENCE. SILENCE. SILENCE. POW! Silence. Silence. More silence. BANG! "Okay, where we at?"

Excellent grouping. A bit high and to the left for me, though. Let's move it about six clicks right and maybe four clicks down. That's should move it an inch and a half to the right and about an inch down. Not bad. Dang, that is a fine rifle and good shooting. BANG! Silence. Silence. Silence. POW! Silence. Silence. Silence. BANG! Suh-weet, only six rounds and she's right on. About three inches high at a hundred yards and you could cover that group with a Montana quarter. That's what we want.

The days are growing shorter now and a detectable fragrance of autumn is in the air. It could be the grain harvest, or the fact that we are now two weeks into the high school football season. Whatever it is, there is something inside every hunter of elk, deer, or antelope that stirs up an indescribable anticipation of the upcoming rifle season. It's not time yet to start putting all your gear together, that'll be two or three weekends from now, but it's definitely time to locate the gun cabinet keys and dust off the hunting rifles.

The tall pine cabinet is in plain sight and has been all year, but now we actually pay earnest attention to it. We find the hidden keys, then unlock and open the glass display doors. Each rifle has its own notch and sits comfortably barrel-up with scope at angle toward the back of the cabinet. An olfactory treat of pine, walnut, leather, gun oil, and solvent greets us as we swing the doors out wide. The scent causes the many autumns past to converge into one synapse in my mind, and I can almost see the faces of my dad, grandpa, and brothers through the frost of an early Montana morning. For that fleeting moment I am transported back to the seemingly carefree and benevolent times of my own youth as a hunter.

I grab the well-used Winchester Model 70 .30-06 Springfield that my father bought for me at Ski's House of Guns twenty-two years ago. To some, that isn't too long ago, but to me it's a relative lifetime. The rifle is only beginning to show its age, where the bluing on the barrel is starting to rub off here and there, with some scratches on the walnut stock. Over the years, it's had different scopes and slings on it, along with trigger work and barrel bedding work, but the main machinery is the same. It's still a fine shooter, capable of downing any North American game animal with a single well-placed shot.

I have one other rifle in there that I'll ensure is sighted in this year. It's a Weatherby Mark V .300 Winchester Mag. In our sighting-in kit we have things like flathead screwdrivers for scope adjustment, zeroing targets and orange hole-markers, a staple gun to put up the targets, a spotting scope and tripod, hearing protection, and a special adjustable rifle rest that aids precise shooting. All of these things we store and transport to the gun range in a brown Cabela's duffel bag.

For some reason, we always go to the gun range on a Sunday, late morning, between NFL games. We'll go only if the air is calm, to ensure precise shots. A tiny bit of coolness is evident as we load the rifles and other gear into the pickup. Some sort of deep and sentimental feeling entrenches itself in me as we conduct this ritual. It's a feeling that won't leave until this season becomes another memory, with Christmas and the New Year arriving on the shoulders of winter.

Two hours or so later and we're all done shooting, back home, and in the den watching the Cowboys play the Giants, running rods down the barrels of our rifles. When finished, we'll put them back in the cabinet until the opening day of deer-hunting season, October 10. Then it's back to the daily grind. Now, though, we each have something brewing in our minds and moving through the calendar. Next task is to get the rest of our gear cleaned and assembled.

It's coming, that first morning. The leaves on the aspens will be changing colors soon, the rest of the land becoming a hunter's tan. No slamming truck doors, no talking out loud. Muffled whispers through the crisp morning air, witnessed only by the creek and the trees and the stars. Autumn has officially arrived with the first crack of the rifle at the gun range.

2—Opening Day

I SPENT LAST NIGHT ENSURING that it was all together and ready to go. I specifically made sure I had my license, tags, rifle, and cartridges, at least one of which I have forgotten to bring in the past, thus cutting the hunt astoundingly short. I also penned a list of gear and stuff onto the back side of a folded piece of notebook paper, and crossed it off as I loaded the essentials into the pickup. I probably had more things than I would need, but as they say, better to have and not need.... The last thing I did was reverse the direction of the truck in the garage; I wanted it nose-out so I could put it in gear and roll out in a hurry, into the pre-dawn darkness.

I may have towed myself and my tent up to the area a day or two in advance and enjoyed some time to chill in the chill before I had to get down to the business of the chase, but this year I was under a time constraint. Opening day of the Idaho mule deer season would be the only day I could sneak away this first full week of October. I swear that I will somehow change this aspect of my life one day, and just make more time to get away to the outdoors in this most wonderful of seasons. Until then, I will certainly make the most of the time I do have, as I did today.

I like to have a partner with whom to share the experience of hunting. My lifelong and best hunting

11

partner is my father, although I expect he will have to cede that designation to my son Will eight or nine seasons from now. Dad has all the qualities that I think make a good hunting partner — superior senses, a good work ethic, a no-nonsense sense of conversation, and a true love of nature. And he is *always* prepared. Still getting excited at the mere utterance of some variation of the phrase "there's one" is also a bonus quality in a hunting partner. After all, if it's not fun, why spend so much money and time doing it?

I picked up Dad at 5:30 a.m. sharp. Record lows they predicted, and this morning's cold proved that up. We've already experienced snow here in the valley this month, so we were dressed in the wool pants — a fashion statement I haven't made on the opening day of deer hunting in six or seven seasons. We jumped on I-15 north and accelerated the gear-laden pickup to a cruising speed of seventy-seven miles an hour. Ahead of us was a steady stream of red-ant taillights disappearing into the northern darkness, while behind us the white-yellow pairs of eyes tried to catch and pass us. We sipped Folgers out of plastic travel mugs and I drifted in memory through a collage of seasons past and of those with whom I'd shared those frosty mornings. Some are still alive, and some have relinquished their souls to heaven and their memories to the ages. They are intangibly present to me, though, and will be passengers in my mind on every opening day.

I am reminded of the popularity of deer hunting in the Birch Creek Valley when I start counting the trailers and wall tents pitched on the bank of the stream, just out of the span of my headlights. There is activity around each one as other families and hunting partners stretch out fold-a-bed stiff knees and air-mattress sore backs. I hope every one of them is as excited as I am about the prospects of the day.

As usual, I miss the turn-off and have to pull a u-turn in the middle of the highway, grabbing gears fast because there are other pickups right on my tail. Then it's a right turn up the dirt road, through the barbed-wire gate, over the foothills, across the draw, up the slope and toward the willows. Before darkness gives way to dawn, I stop the truck and get out to take a stretch, rotate the hubs to locked, and uncase a rifle (hey, can't pass up an easy one). I hang my binocs over my head. Next is a little early morning four-byin' when I have to pull the pickup into four-low and climb a steep two-track.

Now it's dawn and we have reached the snowline. My vision is super-charged. I scan every place a deer might hang out—edges of timber and plateaus, south sides of arroyos, scattered patches of piñon-juniper stands. If *anything* looks out of the ordinary to either of us, I'll stop and we'll get a ten-power zoom-in on it. It's amazing how your mind will take a non-living piece of terrain—like a rock or a stump—and turn it into a deer. This is one reason we examine things with binoculars and not rifle scopes.

We take the east fork of a two-track and crawl over the ruts and rocks to a good parking spot. The moment the engine is stopped, an absolute—and I mean

13

absolute — quiet takes over. We spend a minute or two getting our minds used to it before stepping out and glassing the adjacent terrain. Damn, it isn't thirty seconds and I have spotted some sort of ungulate, about three-quarters of a mile off, making its solitary way across the plain. In this country, it could be a mule deer, an elk, or an antelope, but most likely it's a deer, probably a lone buck. Back in the truck we zip down the two-track through snow patches to intercept the animal.

I slam on the brakes as I see the animal crest the hillock and stop on the skyline, ears up, alerted to our presence. We bring up the binocs and determine it's a doe. If this had been a four-point buck, I would now be slinging 180-grain .300 Winchester Magnums downrange at it, hoping to end its life as swiftly as possible, my human prey-drive taking over. As it stands, though, we just admire the grace of the doe as she trots unalarmed down the shallow slope and one-hops the barbed-wire fence.

When I turn around to head back to the original stopping point, I am amazed at the number of hunters and rigs I can see from this vantage point alone. North of us, across the canyon, are two hunters on foot, four on ATVs, and one in a truck. East of us, a red Chevy makes its way in our direction. Below it on the two-track we drove is a gray Dodge pickup. Over by the big patch of timber a black Suburban sits.

There is a youth season on does up here, but I still hope our doe can get away from this mass of bloodthirsty humanity. Why the paradox? If they do

14

catch her, I hope they shoot straight at least, treat the animal humanely, and use all the meat.

Back at the original parking spot in a small garden of sagebrush, Dad and I gear up to take a little walk. We're going to work a patch of mahogany trees, and meet on the south side near the edge of a draw. We have taken three four-point bucks from this exact spot. With layers of warm clothes on, laced-up Danner boots, and packs with all the necessary gear on our shoulders, we set out, cradling our rifles. It isn't two minutes and I hear *sssssssssst!* It's the universal hunter's signal, indicating the presence of game. I scan the sidehill below and quickly pick up movement about four hundred yards away, easily within range of the Mark V Weatherby I'm packing. My heart is racing and my hands are shaking, despite the fact that I have seen hundreds and hundreds of deer before, and shot probably twenty of them in my life.

There are ten deer. I check the headgear on each one, but cannot grow any bone on the brain. All does and fawns. They gather in a swale below me and I whistle at them just for fun. They look up at me and I stand up and whistle again, then leave Dad and start hunting my way through the patch of trees. I'm on the lookout for the buck who's too smart to be out in the open this morning.

A couple hours later I tie in with Dad again and we compare notes. Nothing, except for that group of does and fawns, and about a dozen different trucks and four-wheelers road hunting. We make our way back to the pickup, still actively scanning the terrain. In just that time, we spot five more does and fawns, startle a coyote, and watch a confused group of ten cow elk and one raghorn bull circle around in the sagebrush prairie far below us.

At the truck, we enjoy a mid-day meal of roast beef sandwiches, pepperoni sticks, Doritos, and cream cheese pastries. With this many hunters rooting around everywhere, we probably stand as much chance of seeing deer from here as anywhere else. The little elk herd has lined out and is making its way toward us. The sun is high in the sky now and warms us through the glass of the pickup windows. A final cup of coffee from the thermos puts the finishing touch on lunch as Dad tells me stories of deer hunts from the past.

We drive slowly back down the dirt road and back onto the state highway, headed south. Dad dozes in the passenger seat and I listen to country music on the radio. In just a few hours we experienced all this, but we don't have to spend the rest of the weekend elbow deep in knives, hide, blood, and bones. Success hunting does not always mean killing. This is my kind of opening day.

3—Anteloping

A NTELOPE HUNTING, OR ANTELOPING, as my friends and I call it, takes place during the surreal seasonal confluence of late summer with early fall. It simply does not get any more perfect in Idaho for outdoor activities. The high of the previous summer is only faintly seasoned with the melancholy sentiment of anticipating an upcoming winter. Late September is glorious, and with antelope tag in hand, you are one of the relative few fortunate enough to experience an Idaho high-desert September, and to have a purpose while doing it.

Ostensibly, you're out here to put meat on the table — fill your tag. Antelope, though some consider it too gamey tasting, is a meat my family considers a near delicacy. In reality, and in my mind at least, that "fill-the-tag" part is only a small fraction of why I'm here. Yes, it's a very, very exciting fraction, but it's also an inevitable segue to a mildly sad and confusing time when you realize you just killed a beautiful wild animal. And then there's a bunch of work to do, especially if you butcher the animal yourself.

Mostly, though, I cherish moments spent wandering in no particular fashion to an only roughly-defined destination in a sea of sagebrush. A month ago, I might have been out here chasing a smoke from a lightning strike — hell bent on adrenaline, and talking on the two-way radio with other firefighters with the same mindset. Now I have no goal except to avoid too much adrenaline. I am out here alone to appreciate the calm, and to appreciate my small-ness in the world.

The light-blue dawn and the Morningstar give way to a blood-red horizon in the east. There is not even a hint of a breeze and the only sound on the entire prairie is my careful footsteps and the occasional brush of my denim pant leg on sagebrush. It is so quiet that if you don't consciously concentrate on not concentrating, the silence can turn into a faint ringing in your ears. Sometimes this faint ringing makes me think that at any moment all hell could break loose and bullets will fly. The utter silence has certainly been a harbinger of action in the past.

As I've grown older and more mature in my thoughts about hunting, I've noticed a distinct shift in goals — from being bloodthirsty when I was ten, eleven, or twelve-ish, to a more overall appreciation of the overall hunt — to the point of even being thankful for the opportunity and ability to hunt. I'd be lying to you, though, if I told you I didn't want to get some shooting or see some action today. I guarantee I will be nervous, shaking, and full of adrenaline if I spot an antelope; and orders of magnitude more keyed-up should the opportunity for shooting arise. Just thinking of the possibility makes me shake a little. Yes, I love all of it, even the shooting.

I walk in a crouch as I come over a rise; it isn't good to silhouette yourself on a skyline. On the north side of the low ridge I find a good spot to hunker down just above some short junipers. First I pick a good boulder on which to set my pack. I'll use the pack for a rifle rest. Swiveling on the pack will allow me to point the rifle's muzzle in a large arc to the left and to the right, depending on where the antelope come from.

And they will come. I have sat in nearly this same spot on three other antelope hunts, and on each one of those, antelope have walked through the same saddle 100 yards across from me on a game trail. When I was twelve, on my first-ever antelope hunt, I think every antelope in the valley came through single-file in a line that must have stretched for a quarter mile. I got so excited that I stood right up and started banging away wildly. One shot went straight up in the air, another hit the dirt six feet in front of me. One of the shots at the now-racing herd connected with a small doe and she crumpled. I had to walk up and shoot her again. I cried. On the other two hunts I kept my composure and was able to make one-shot kills.

Now I just sit motionless and hope the sun will hurry up and warm me up. It's still completely silent, but if I listen carefully, past the faint ringing, I can hear cars passing now and then on Highway 28 in the distance. Although nothing is moving, I take out my binoculars and scan up and down some sagebrush draws and across the prairie below me. An interesting thing happens when you're hunting, and it must be an ancient adaptation—your vision and hearing become extremely keen. Every boulder becomes an animal, and even the slightest of noises is amplified. Experience tells me, after I've finished my binocular

19

scan, that nothing is here yet. Anticipation and that perfect stillness and the faint ringing in my ears. Action is in the air. I feel it on my skin. I check my rifle's chamber to make sure it's ready. I wait for the sun to come up and an antelope to come over the hill.

When it finally doesn't seem that it could get any quieter, I look to my left across the swale and up the low ridge. There is buck antelope standing there, alone. It's a mystery to me how game animals just sometimes appear. They are not there, and then they're there. I could see it was a buck before I put the scope on him because of the prominent black sideburns that a pronghorn male has. I decide to take this one.

Sitting a bit lower down in the dirt, I slowly and simultaneously adjust my body and the rifle until it's almost like we've become one. One killing machine. The buck appears in my scope quartered toward me. I have my Winchester Model 70, so I must thumb the safety two clicks forward to the "Fire" position. Now I take a deep breath, let out half of it, and try to center the crosshairs on the buck's chest as I squeeze the trigger.

"BANG"

The flat crack of the rifle is so startling in this otherwise peaceful setting. I guess you kind of expect more of a deeper "boom" sound than that "crack." It makes a quick echo across the draw and then it's silent again. The antelope, not knowing where the shot came from, walks two steps forward and stops broadside to me.

"BANG" — another miss.

20

The antelope still stands broadside to me. I decide I am shooting over him, so I adjust my aim accordingly and squeeze off a third shot. To write it so calmly like this doesn't give justice to the combination of nerves with determination I felt right then.

"BANG-WHAP" — this sound is the unmistakable sound of a bullet hitting flesh. The antelope turned and ran crouched, but at full speed, down the low ridge. I assumed he was hit hard, but not wanting to risk losing him, I shot a fourth time.

"BANG-WHAP"

This time the antelope went down for good.

It's a smart practice at this point to just sit for a bit and calm down. While doing so, I inserted four new 150-grain rounds into the rifle's magazine and took a swig of cold water from my canteen. My eyes never left the downed antelope.

So much had just happened — so much noise and violence and change — yet it was absolutely silent on the prairie as the world continued on. How is this? The sun wasn't even fully in the sky, and I had caused this, and the hunt was essentially over.

I found the buck lying stretched out in the dried prairie grass near an outcrop of volcanic rocks. I really don't ever know what to think at this point, or how exactly to feel. Should I be back-slapping joyful, or sad, or a combination maybe? It's weird; usually I just feel melancholy at the thought of how suddenly life can end. This reinforces the fact that there are no second acts or encores. There is one life. Saying out loud "thank you antelope—for giving your life so that mine continues on" doesn't work for me, so I don't do that.

Soon enough, thought is replaced with action as I initiate the act of processing this animal into food. I field dress it (pull out the guts), and because the carcass needs to cool quickly, skin it right there. Then I wrap said carcass in cheesecloth and haul it back to the truck for the ride home.

By now, the sun is high in the sky. There are airplane contrails up there, and dust trails from other hunters' pickups down here. I sip a Diet Coke and eat a couple of chocolate chip cookies as I bounce out of the drainage on the dirt road. "That was pretty easy," I think to myself, considering how hard I usually have to work to fill a tag.

Then I turn onto the blacktop highway and head south. Thinking it means more to me than saying it, especially to an entity committed by me to eternity. Thank you, Antelope.

4—Bloodthirsty

A S WITH EVERYTHING, there is a first time — and so it goes for big-game hunting. The best way, I think, to introduce a kid to hunting is with a BB gun and some pop cans, or beer cans. Bottles make a mess, so it's probably best to avoid those. Hundreds and hundreds of BB's later and the kid hopefully knows that when you point a gun at something and pull the trigger, some kind of destruction occurs, so they start to learn to be concerned about where that gun is pointing.

A side story I have to add to this, as an apology to my dad and a warning to other dads, is about the time my brother and I got hold of our BB guns when no adults were home. We started by shooting at cans, and paper targets with animals drawn on them, but for some reason that got boring, so we proceeded to shoot out all of my dad's boat trailer lights. I'll never forget how cool it looked and sounded when that first BB thunked right through the center of that fat red left taillight. And then it was game-on, I mean we shot out every light and reflector. And then when all those were broken, I thought we were going to replace our barn someday anyway, so I shot out every perfectly good window on the barn. What an asshole kid. The moral of that story, I suppose, is to keep *every* gun locked up.

So then you move on to the .22 rifle. I think every household in America ought to have at least a .22 rifle, for training if nothing else. I learned on a Winchester Model 06 pump-action .22 rifle. This is an old-school gun, but it worked just perfectly (and like the BB gun, I still have it). We took that rifle on every camping trip we ever went on, and out to the desert west of town as often as we had time. We started on the same kind of targets as the BB gun—cans and paper plates and stuff. And after a couple months doing that, we would start to look for jackrabbits to shoot. I am basically an animal lover, and I have never really liked to kill things, but I do sometimes believe jackrabbits and rockchucks—yellow-bellied marmots—were put on Earth for eagles and coyotes to eat and for kids to practice marksmanship. I think in between the ages of six and twelve I hunted thirty times for those and shot a total of two.

At age eleven, I took the state hunter safety course. This is an excellent, in-class, hands-on, four-evening training course in the ways of safe and responsible hunting, especially as it pertains to the ways of the gun. If you pass the in-class and rifle-range tests, you get that card. I still have mine, and because I was born after January 1, 1975, I still have to present it every time I buy a hunting license. It's more important to me than my social security card, which I haven't seen for years!

And then because it's America, and because I was fortunate enough to have a very generous father, the time comes when you get your own big-game hunting rifle, which sometimes happens before you go on your first big-game hunt. I suppose it'd be okay to borrow another family member's rifle, but the idea here is that you find a rifle that fits you and you get used to handling it. The more familiar you are with that rifle, the better you can shoot it. My dad still hunts with the same rifle he bought when he was twelve years old, a Remington Model 721 .30-06.

My choices were boiled down to a Remington Model 700 Mountain Rifle versus a Winchester Model 70 XTR Sporter, both in .30-06 Springfield. I'm not sure if I wanted the .30-06, or was prompted toward that caliber by my dad. I mean, it's perfectly fine for anything you ever wanted to hunt in Idaho and Montana, but, well it's just kind of boring. So I picked the Winchester, only to wish a few hours later that I had picked the Remington. This is a situation I am still trying to make peace with today. My dad also bought a Bushnell fixed 4X scope for it. My dad is generous, but that generosity has its limits. I'm grateful, but that has limits as well. I really wanted to have a Remington BDL in 7mm Remington Magnum or a Winchester Model 70 in .270 Weatherby Magnum, the latter of which I don't think they manufacture anymore—and either of which I wanted to top with a Leupold Vari-X scope, but what right do beggars have? I promise I wasn't as entitled a little shit as I'm making out, it's just that I had just read way too many *Outdoor Life* magazines and gun catalogs by the time I was twelve.

So it was September and I sat in the secret spot I'm just going to start calling "Antelope Pass" because it's where the antelope always pass through. A starry night gave way to a beautiful but frigid dawn, and I sat physically motionless amongst the tall sagebrush while my mind ran around and around. I am a dreamer and a pretender, so I can pass a lot of time thinking up various scenarios and how I'd react. Sometimes I'd even make myself believe I'm cooler than I really am and I would make up little stories in my mind about what happened and what I did. I was probably sitting there telling myself a little story about how I shot the biggest buck as it walked through Antelope Pass. One shot, one kill. I would even make little gunshot noises with my mouth and watch with my mind's eye what happened after I shot. If I wasn't doing that, I would've been thinking about different kinds of rifles I might have been carrying right then if I was in charge of the world.

No doubt this was what I was doing for the three or four hours I sat in the sagebrush, when I looked to my left and here came an antelope, then another, and another, and another. So much for the cool dude! My heart immediately raced and I began to shake. I shouldered my rifle, which I hadn't quite grown into yet or learned to be comfortable with, and I looked through the scope. All I could see were heads and the tops of backs as this huge herd paraded by just fifty yards below my position. There were does and fawns and wall-hanger bucks, and medium bucks, and small bucks, and bucks with a wide spread of horns and does with horns and every damn size and shape of antelope you could imagine. The fucking sagebrush

26

was too tall and I couldn't get good eye-relief on my scope, so there was a black spot partially covering up my scope's field of view, and though they weren't running, they weren't waiting around either. Why is it never like I planned or dreamed!?

So I just stood straight up. Antelope aren't gonna hang around in that situation, and they can run fifty-five miles an hour. A bloodthirsty twelve-year-old boy isn't gonna wait for some kind of better situation than this, so I opened fire. And I mean opened fire. I shot wildly over and under and around the racing herd, never aiming, just pointing and working the bolt. I remember a large dust cloud as the antelope were bugging out. When you're that ripped on adrenaline, time slows down, but the whole thing couldn't have lasted more than thirty seconds or maybe even half that.

Only the dust cloud lingered, and my ears were ringing. There were no antelope in sight—dead, wounded, or fully alive. I screamed cusswords and hated myself for screwing this up. What an epic chance and an equally epic failure. But it was the antelope's fault really, and my dad's, and my rifle's, and even God's fault. Not my fault. Because it didn't play out like I had planned, it could never be my fault. That's an angry twelve-year-old boy's thoughts. I sat heavily back into the dirt and cried failure tears and clenched my fists.

My dad, though, had watched the whole thing go down, including an antelope. Antelope Pass has a natural set of bleachers about a half mile away to the east, in an outcrop of rocks down the slope and across the two-track road. Dad had sat there all morning reading a book, until the movement of a hundred or so antelope caught his eye. He had watched as they crossed into my view, watched as I stood up in the sagebrush, and then watched as dust was kicked up by wild .30-06 rounds, the ka-POW of the rifle report reaching his ears moments after seeing the shot. The herd continued to run past me and over the low ridge, resembling the stock market ticker at the bottom of the TV when you're tuned to the all-news channels. Dad saw a flash of white as an antelope rolled away from the herd and went down from a delayed reaction. Antelope run so damn fast that in the timeframe of a moment's delay, this particular antelope covered nearly fifty yards.

So it fell upon Dad to tell me that I had hit one, and it fell upon me to walk up to a spot ten feet away from the little still-alive doe and shoot her once more behind the ear. The first shot had broken both hips. This sucks. This is not how you want it to go down, but it does happen, and the end result is that we retrieved our game and the animal didn't go to waste. I learned one of the most important lessons that day, though, and that's to always check for a blood trail and/or look for a wounded or dead animal lying hidden in the brush after you shoot. That actually happens fairly often; an animal will run for a bit even after being hit fatally. So you go look for a blood trail. Always. I wish I could say I learned to calm down at the moment of truth, but that wouldn't come for many more years.

5—Montana Muleys, the Way It Was

ON OUR TRIPS TO MONTANA, I always pretended that ground blizzards in the distance were herds of caribou running this way as we drove up I-15 at four in the morning. I pretended the Ford Bronco was a helicopter and we were watching these caribou scatter out in front of us the way you see it on *National Geographic* and *Wild America* and other such shows. It seemed like there were a lot more jackrabbits back then too, and they were always running out into the road in front of us. Once I asked my dad why he didn't try harder to run them over, and his response was that he was worried a bone might puncture a tire. I know now that this response was just to shut me up. The real reason is that he is a mature individual and is not going to risk wrecking the truck trying to hit a damn rabbit, and also that he's not into killing just for the sake of killing.

I came of age in the hunting world at the apex of the old-school way. I came of age when the guys still wore red and black-checkered plaid wool and you had to get out of the truck to lock in the hubs for the four-wheel drive. I don't think many hunters used rifles with stocks made of composite materials then. This was late '70s, early '80s era hunting. A lot of people think even the weather was harsher then. I guess, anecdotally at least, that I would have to agree with that because on these Thanksgiving Day hunting trips we used to make, it seems like I always remember a bunch of snow on the ground, even in town, and big flakes and big drifts all the way over Monida Pass into Montana. Of course, the old-timers also maintain that there was more game then, too, but I'm not sure if I really agree with that.

In reality, we probably made only three or four of these Thanksgiving Day hunts as a generational family unit, but the few trips made such an impression on me that they stick in my memory black-box as if we made them all the time. The fuzzy and intangible part of this composite three-or-four-year story is not in the deer we killed, but in the mixture of personalities that crammed into the Bronco at four in the morning, and oddly enough, how the personalities paired with the rifles each guy (or kid) brought.

I couldn't even sleep the night before we'd leave; I was even more excited than Christmas Eve. My minimal gear included a coat, mittens, a stocking cap, and a BB gun and they were ready and loaded way before anyone else's. I even remember one year converting my school backpack into a hunting pack and putting a pocket knife, toy binoculars, and extra BB's into it. My dad's stuff would be ready next—and though he was *the* hunter of all of us, he was the only one who wouldn't bring a rifle; acting more as a guide on these trips than a principal participant. Grandpa wore wool from head to toe, inside to outside, and an old pair of leather-on-top, rubber-on-the-bottom Pac boots. He had had a stroke a decade before and wasn't too ambulatory anymore, so for symbolic purposes, if nothing else, we threw in a bull-barreled custom-built 6mm Remington for him to shoot, just in case there happened to be a deer that wanted to kill itself that day. It had a huge twelve-power scope on it and no sling. The thing weighed probably fifteen pounds and no hunter would ever have hiked with a rifle like that. But Gramps *was* the only one of us who had a resident Montana hunting license, so he probably ought to have a rifle.

With my brother Tom and one of his fine mule deer from the Sheep Creek country

Stan, my oldest brother, and Tom, my middle brother, were primarily concerned with things that didn't relate to hunting. Stan, somewhere between seventeen and twenty-one those years, cared only about girls. Tom, somewhere between nine and thirteen, cared mostly about his friends and football. Though hunting was all I cared about then, to them it was at best something possibly semi-exciting, and at worst, an annoyance taking away from sleep and social time. They would have probably used any gear that you gave them, including a rifle. Stan was given a J.C. Higgins Model 50 rifle sometime in his early teens. My dad's uncle had converted it from a .270 Winchester into an ear-splitting and probably not much ballistically improved .270 Weatherby Magnum, with a trigger so light that if you even looked at it wrong it would touch off. One hunt, though, actually the one I remember most clearly, Stan brought my dad's Remington Model 760 slide-action .30-06 instead. This was because Stan had "accidentally" dropped the .270 and broke the stock. Tom and I knew better than that, though. We knew he had a temper and most likely had grabbed it by the barrel and smashed it into the ground or wrapped it around a tree trunk. Tom had a Winchester Model 70 in .243 — a fine little rifle — and of course Tom hated it.

I sat in the middle of the back seat of the Bronco, Stan to my left, Tom to my right, and Grandpa riding shotgun and mumbling about anything and everything. Once in awhile you'd hear Stan, not quite under his breath, whisper, "I wish he'd just shut the fuck up."

The snow "caribou" and the snowplows, along with the snow piled high on the sides of the highway, reminded you that you were going hunting, and you'd probably better enjoy the warmth of the Bronco and the hot chocolate because your ass was gonna be out in that cold before too long. I just sat and imagined various scenarios about what deer we'd see and the action that would go down.

Gramps freezing in the Big Hole. It's so cold
you couldn't hear him say "ya can't eat tracks!"

I was too young to hunt on these trips, except for on the very last one we made, but that didn't matter, I still had my BB gun and dreams along. I even made those little gun noises with my mouth until once when Tom told me to shut the fuck up. I was embarrassed about those noises after that—I still made them, but only in private.

At Lima, we exited the interstate and headed west across a sagebrush flat. The wind had died down now and the anticipation had ramped up. Outside of the headlights it was pitch dark, but in my mind I saw the patches of timber we'd glass and I wondered where the deer were. There was no more talking inside the vehicle. I bet even Stan might have been a little excited at this point, even though he was still feigning sleep. There was a fork in the road where we veered left and at this point the sagebrush was taller than the Bronco;

the back end of the truck shimmied around in the snow ruts. At the head of Little Sheep Creek it was time to shut down the engine, uncase the rifles, and wait for shooting light, fifteen or twenty minutes, maybe. Grandpa and Stan would switch places, and the five of us were alone—silent but for Grandpa's occasional low mumbling.

The sun rose up from behind us, so the tops of the ridges were the first geological features that turned from invisible to silhouettes to earth parts with tan or white color, depending on the volume of snow that had stayed or been blown into drifts. Then the patches of timber shifted from invisible to black to dark green—and stayed that way unless you were close enough to any of them that they turned that evergreen color. It was going to be a windless but crisp blue-sky day, and pretty soon every goddamn thing you looked at was a deer. Every stump and rock and dead tree looked like a mule deer. That's your mind on full hunting focus. Some people never get over this and they end up seeing stuff that really isn't there, or isn't what it appears to be. So they end up accidentally shooting their hunting partner as he hikes up the hill because he bent over for a second and looked like a nice four-point buck. Everywhere you look near the truck, when you step out to take a piss, are deer tracks. Then there's the inevitable comment from Grandpa, "Ya can't eat tracks." Every year.

You aren't legally supposed to road hunt, but don't give me that baloney, everyone does. Especially back in the day like that when you had a nice long canyon like this one to drive, glassing the slopes with your binocs. You'd never be able to cover enough country walking, so you do a little of what we here in the West call "four-bying." The term means to put to use all the power of your four-by-four vehicle and churn through the snow up the road that traverses the south slope of the canyon. Eyes and mind focused and on full power, you scan the sidehills and gulches and the edges of the small patches of timber.

Make no mistake about Grandpa, he may be old and not moving very fast, and he mumbles too much in the early mornings, but he makes up for it with experience and eagle eyes. "Hup! There we go!" he exclaims as he spots a buck leading two does up a gulch to our right, headed south, about to cross the road two hundred yards in front of us. The buck has at least four points on each antler (east of the Mississippi they would call this an eight-point; in the west, it's a four-point). Then when we look closer, the second doe is actually a "forkhorn" buck. Forkhorn (or forked-horn or even forky) is slang for a buck with two points on each antler. And then we see that there are more than two does following the buck, looks like nine or ten actually, all bounding through this gulch with only a few sparse juniper bushes.

Non-resident Montana hunting licenses aren't cheap and my dad had bought one for himself, one for Stan, and one for Tom. Dad is from Montana and couldn't bear to give up hunting in that state. But Stan did not give a shit about who paid for what and for how much. This is business to him, and the business is getting deer on the ground and in the truck, and back to Idaho Falls just as soon as we can. Stan was not going to wait around for everyone to wrestle with themselves and struggle past straps and ropes and latches and jump out of the truck and get into position.

BANG! Bullets already in the air as that lead buck bounded across the road and up the other sidehill. Now it's crumpled and rolling back down that hill— legs and basket-rack and head flopping everywhere. POW! The forkhorn buck drops in its tracks, courtesy of the same rifle that dropped the four-point. Now there are 180-grain silvertips flying out to fill the one doe tag we have. Snow and dirt fly up in front of and behind her as the last two rounds in the magazine narrowly miss. A couple of inches higher and to the right with that third shot and we'd have three mule deer on the ground.

When we look back at the four-point he is up again, evidently not realizing he is dead. Stan drops the magazine clip out of the 760, pulls a loaded spare one from his left pocket and slaps that one in place—four more 180-grain bullets. It takes only two though, and the deed is done. The four-point began to angle back up the sidehill, hit hard anyway, and then Stan put two more shots in the firebox and the buck was down for good.

All this happened before the rest of us had even bailed out of the truck. If Stan had had his way, he would have filled everyone's tag right then and there, but as it turned out, we had only the four-point and the forkhorn bucks on the ground, ready to be field-dressed. The rest of the herd we could still see trotting over the skyline to our left, about a thousand yards away at this point.

Not bad for fifteen minutes of hunting. But we still had one more buck tag and one more doe tag to fill, and this was going to be the last day we'd be hunting this season.

My family always made good use of our wild-game meat, and my dad and grandpa were not the kind of guys who liked to leave tags unfilled in those days, so I knew this day was far from over.

I was twelve when I went on my first of these Thanksgiving hunts as a licensed hunter. I was not aware of it then, but my dad paid a lot of money for us to carry these out-of-state permits. I kind of wish I'd been more appreciative then, but all I cared about at that age was seeing, shooting, and killing whatever I had a permit for.

Kind of like the vestiges of a rock'n'roll band who still tour under that name when half the members have moved on, it was only Dad, Grandpa, and I sitting three across in the '74 GMC pickup at the base of the same canyon several years later. Stan had passed away tragically two years before, and Tom had more or less moved on to new hobbies. Each of us sat in the silence of the truck, and I am wondering now what Dad and Grandpa were thinking about. Were they remembering the old times, which are almost always better, or at least simpler, when contemplated retrospectively? Were they just wanting to get the day done and make a good time for me? Gramps didn't mumble anymore, he just looked through the windshield and rested his leather-mittened hand on my knee, once in awhile giving it a squeeze. Dad chewed gum and still seemed to be mostly businesslike, but once in awhile I would catch what may have been a wistful look on his face.

I was not melancholy, or retrospective, in any way in those days. I was twelve and still bloodthirsty. I had performed awfully so far as a legal hunter. There was the doe antelope incident, and then on the opening day of the Idaho deer season, same year, it took twenty-two rounds from the same rifle to bag a 3x2 buck mule deer. With twenty-two rounds, I hit it only once, in the back right leg. The poor bastard lay down in a patch of junipers and I had to have my dad go in and finish it off because I had just two bullets left and I didn't want to screw it up. We had taken my dad's friend Frank with us that day, and he told me he was worried that World War III had started because he had heard so much shooting coming from my direction. I was hoping today to find a path to a sportsman's redemption, and though I may have wished my two brothers were with us, and that things were the way they'd been before, all I really wished was that I might get some shooting today. I even had little nerve chills thinking about it as the sun rose slowly in the east and the landscape shifted its colors.

6—The Mine Gulch

O N MY DAD'S WALL, THERE ARE THREE giant mule deer bucks whose marble eyes watch every move you make when you're there in the basement. Two of them have really dark gray hair, and those boys are the ones from Montana, from the same gulch, taken years apart. Dad still tells the stories from those hunts, and I still listen, though maybe not as eagerly as I did as a kid.

Mule deer taxidermy mounts in my dad's basement. The buck on the left was taken by my oldest brother Stan in southeast Idaho; the other two are from the Mine Gulch in southwest Montana.

I remember diverting from the traditional Sheep Creek Thanksgiving Day hunt one year and traveling through Twin Bridges and Sheridan and finally Alder to this hunting spot. The most profound memory on this hunt was the two lines of blood running down either side of the bridge of Grandpa's nose after the

39

scope on the 6mm bit him. You see, at the top of the fairly thick-timbered canyon there's what I call now the "shooting gallery." It's where the deer would funnel through after someone pushed them out from the timber below. If you had three hunters, one guy went up one side of the canyon, one guy went up the other side of the canyon, and the third (the short straw) would bust up the center and make all kinds of noise to move any deer that are hanging out in there. This guy is the "driver."

That day Tom and I stayed with Grandpa at the truck while Dad and Stan worked the canyon. Without a driver, Stan and Dad just went up either side of the canyon in hopes that eventually the deer would funnel into the shooting gallery on their own as the day progressed. Well, an hour or so after daylight, Gramps got the idea that he could act as a driver from a thousand yards below with the 6mm. Without a word, he levered himself out of the truck, uncased the 6mm, and using his cane to stabilize himself, cut loose into the timber with a four-or-five-round salvo. "That oughta get 'em movin." And he struggled back into the truck with Tom and me wide-eyed and giggling.

A few hours later, when Dad and Stan were back at the truck, my Dad asked him, "What the hell were you shooting at down here?"

Evidently they hadn't quite reached the spot that was within range of deer coming through the shooting gallery when Grandpa opened up, so each of them could only watch with binoculars from their respective side of the canyon when a dozen or so does and a

40

monster buck trotted through the gallery and down the other side — into a jungle of timber. The only blood drawn that day was that which ran down the sides of Grandpa's nose from the scope bite. The best thing about Gramps, though, is he didn't give a shit; it seemed right to him at the time, so he didn't feel a bit bad. In fact, he probably thought it was pretty funny.

I often leave my spent cartridges up in the mountains, at the very place I jacked them out of the rifle after I shot. It's my way of leaving a mark that I hunted there, and I don't consider it littering — though in some cases I've left behind enough cases at a single spot that it looks like a gun range — and that would be one of those days that I had had buck fever. I kind of think of these spent casings like arrowheads, in that there's probably a good story attached to each one. Since I've done this, I've been able to go back to those places, and in a couple of instances even found the casings again. In my memory I was transported instantly back to that time, sometimes even with a tear in my eye.

In the Mine Gulch, in 1988, I sat under a juniper bush on the north side of the shooting gallery. I was cold and nervous — and shivering from a combination of the two stimuli. Again on this trip, it was just the vestiges of the rock'n'roll band, with Grandpa waiting down at the truck. Dad was the driver and I could hear him in the canyon below cracking timber loudly to push some deer out. This was such a good spot that I was already thinking about sending some deer jerky to my Grandpa's brother Robie, a World War II Navy veteran who lived in Garden Grove, California, and who ate only jerky and drank only beer — pounds and gallons respectively. It was obvious to me in my twenties that I was related to him.

I scanned far and near and all around me, making up sounds in my ears and huge buck deer in my eyes. One of those little furry chipmunks ran across a dead piece of juniper log below me. As I looked at it, I could see something out of place, so I scooted a few feet down the hill and found three .270 Weatherby Magnum casings, tarnished from many years in the weather. There was only one person that could have left them there, and with a quick mental calculation, I knew it had been at least a decade since my brother had sat in this same spot. He was long gone by then, but not really gone at all. Does this mean you live forever if you're remembered?

It's still possible to make decent shots through scopes with watery eyes. It's always windy on the north side of the shooting gallery where you're kind of exposed. If you keep still, though, the deer *always* come out and funnel through that little saddle. You have about a minute and a half to decide what you're gonna do, because the deer aren't usually galloping across that opening. They're just kind of moving with a purpose. The third or fourth one out was a decent 3x4 buck that came out 25 or 30 yards above the does, as bucks often do. Then I added two or three of my own spent cases to the pile — these were .30-06 shells, and even though there's a lot of hunters who use a .30-06 compared with users of .270 Weatherby Magnums, I hope somebody sees them someday, like I saw my brother's shells. And I hope that person knows those are my .30-06 shells, and the person is someone who loved me and has good memories of me.

My oldest brother Stan with a nice mule deer buck he bagged with the custom-made .270 Weatherby Magnum rifle

7—The Big Hole

THE BIG HOLE VALLEY IS ONE OF Montana's finest treasures. As with most valleys I suppose, this one is named after the river that runs through it. The river's name was originally the Wisdom River, coined by Lewis and Clark in respect of the three cardinal virtues embodied by President Jefferson. The other two virtues—and rivers—were The Philosophy and The Philanthropy, now the Beaverhead River and Ruby River, respectively. The name Wisdom stuck for the town nearest where we hunt. The town is famous in my mind because in my days of pretending I was a cowboy and rancher, Connelly Sporting Goods was where I bought my stuff, and it was on the streets of Wisdom where I got into all my gunfights and fistfights. And speaking of fights, the nearby Big Hole Battlefield is the historical site of one of the turning points of the Nez Perce War. On August 9, 1877 the Nez Perce were camped at this site, and were attacked by U.S. Cavalry troops. After a bloody battle, almost 90 Nez Perce were dead, along with 31 of the soldiers who had attacked them. The Nez Perce and friends gather at the battlefield—now managed by the National Park Service—each summer to commemorate the site and memorialize ancestors who fought and died there. Between June and October of 1877, Chief Joseph, Chief Looking Glass, Chief White Bird, Chief

Ollokot, and Chief Lean Elk led about 750 Nez Perce men, women, and children (and twice that many horses) nearly 1,200 miles through the mountains, from their homeland in northeast Oregon across Idaho and Montana to the Canadian border. A few escaped to Canada, but most were relocated to prison camps in Kansas and Oklahoma.

Haystacks and grazing cattle in the valley now are abundant, and the elk in the nearby Pioneer Mountains are plentiful, too. For my dad and his hunting buddies, the deep dark woods produced regular success, in terms of actually harvesting elk. Stan even shot a nice 5-point bull in there one year, but Tom and I thought this hunting spot sucked. I realized nearly two decades later that Tom and I were quite mistaken in our assessment of this collection of drainages. The place takes patience to hunt, and I sure wouldn't want to be an outfitter in that country, because more often than not you're going to go home empty-handed. Tom and I, and I'm sure many other hunters, have had some epic failures in that country, in more ways than just missing shots.

In all my years of hunting there, I have not once turned off Highway 43 and headed east down that forest road in the daylight. Two-thirds of those times it has been so bum-pissing cold that the little snow crystals are reflecting the moonlight, and the steam from your breath actually has measurable mass. Three-fourths of the times I have turned off there, I've been so tired my head was drooping and dropping and my eyes would sizzle when I blinked those long, long blinks. Two-fifths of the time I have been so hung over that I just wanted to barf through that first cattle guard into the ditch below. Nine-tenths of the time I have been stuffed full from a huge rare steak from Barclay's the night before and from a dozen pancakes that Grandma cooked for me at 3 a.m. So why do I, nearly twenty years removed from these rugged memories, want so badly to go back? Redemption.

To tell you the truth, this is only place I have ever hunted that I thought was a little spooky. This is because of all the stories my dad has told me, and it's because it's so damn dark and thick in there, and it's because you become so alone with your thoughts so fast that you feel like you are watching a movie of your life inside your mind. Then just when you thought you could be no more alone and that there are absolutely no elk here, you will realize that you were not *living in the present*, and thus have fucked up and jumped the bull you were so painstakingly tracking. It is par for the course in this country, at least for me.

When the road makes a hairpin turn and switches back toward the south it's time to park and walk. There's a permanently gated-off logging road here that's full of saplings trying for their own redemption. When I was little, my dad told me that one time, just after he softly clicked the truck door closed and started hiking up that road in the pitch dark, there was a loud "woof" followed by some timber crashing. That damn story has stuck in my head to where it needs a psychiatrist to pry it loose. Every time I sidle past that gate in the dreadful silence and darkness, I'm fully expecting to get mauled by a bear. It's the only place in the world where I'm actually scared of bears. But I also have the dangerous capability of telling myself "fuck it," so I continue down that logging road — and I have done so both alone and with my dad and/or Tom, neither of whom are afraid of anything.

The logging road meanders through the timber for a quarter-mile or so, and when we hunt it, we leave the road here and simply churn straight up the side hill through a pair of sagebrush clearings (we call them parks) that serve as an evidence locker reminding you that the place is full of elk. Elk shit and elk tracks are *everywhere*, easy to see even in the semi-darkness. Although I have never seen a live elk in either of these parks, my dad arrived late here one morning and missed a shot at a 6-point bull. Still, since my brain is piqued and in full hunting mode, everything looks like an elk. My frosty breathing obscures the view and annoys me, but still I scan the park with my rifle scope, because it gathers more light than just the naked eye. At the top of the parks we catch our breath and start looking for a suspect elk track. The track we're looking for is bigger than the others, and usually goes off on its own shortly after entering the timber, though sometimes it's joined by one or two others. The track we're looking for belongs to a bull, and we hope it's a giant one. Sometimes the tracks will simply follow the North Fork trail, and as I start up the trail, the first of the memories hits me.

It may have been four summers before, or five, but we took our horses on their first pack trip up this path,

48

our destination a small clearing on a small stream that follows the Hiline Trail. It was Dad, Tom, and me. Dad put Tom in charge of *one* thing in preparation for this trip, and that was filling the canteens with water. Tom used the bathroom sink to fill the canteens—all with softened water. I don't know if you've ever tried to drink soft water, but it's gross. It works well for showering, but it just seems like you're drinking saltwater, and it makes you thirstier. We had two canteens, both full of soft water, so essentially we had no water. We did have two cans of warm Pepsi, but Tom and I, being quintessential piss-ants, had drunk both of those down while Dad got the horses ready.

When we got to the clearing, hours later and parched, all I cared about was starting a fire to cook and eat hot dogs. I was a fat kid, so every event for me revolved around eating—Thanksgiving Turkey, Easter Ham, Christmas Cookies, Birthday Pizza and Cake, and of course Camping Ball Park (plump when you cook 'em) Hot Dogs and s'mores. So while Dad and Tom did what was supposed to be done to set up a good horse camp, I pulled out a huge and razor-sharp KA-BAR knife and began to whittle down hot dog sticks. I was about two strokes into this when the blade slipped on a knot in the stick and went through my ankle rather like a sharp knife through butter. Tom had watched the whole thing, and instead of "Oh, are you okay?" it was "How deep is it?" in the most exasperated of tones. Then Dad saw it and instead of "Oh, are you okay?" it was "That's why you don't fuck around when you're supposed to be working." And so

49

it goes. We didn't even end the trip early; I just hobbled around with a piece of T-shirt wrapped around my ankle for four days. To make matters worse, I had one of those permanent wire retainers that the orthodontist puts on your lower teeth, and one side broke loose on day two, so I had a piece of wire flopping around my mouth for the duration of the "vacation."

Summer pack trip in the Big Hole

On another of these summer scouting/horse trips, we had gone as the vestiges of a nuclear family, only to scream and yell at one another the whole time. Maybe this is what they mean by a "nuclear" family? We had brought our two dogs with us, one of which was a very fit and fast and clever and gluttonous Basset Hound; she broke into the cooler while we were prepping the camp and ate *five* raw rib steaks. Later on this trip, we lost her when we left the trail and spent hours searching through the timber. We found her huddled under a spruce tree and shivering. She would have been coyote bait in a matter of hours.

Those are the first crystal-clear memories I recall as I pick a track and plod slowly through soft knee-deep snow up the trail behind the set of elk tracks. The track will continue on for several hundred yards before it veers north of the trail into the ratsass of timber we call the North Fork Bowl. After this the memories become more vague and my thoughts more general. Am I young now, or older? A little boy, a punk teenager, or a man?

My first experience as a licensed Montana non-resident hunter in the Big Hole ended in astonishing failure when I missed a nearly point-blank shot at a raghorn bull. I had tracked him all day, so slowly that I may have gone only a half-mile in six or seven hours. My dad had been following my tracks, as I was too young to be left completely alone in that country. He finally caught up to me, began talking out loud because it was time to head back, and kept that one-sided conversation going even as I hissed (almost like you do in nightmare), "There he is Dad, there he is!" or something like that. Why I didn't bring up my goddamn rifle and shoot is still a mystery to me, but by the time I slowly brought the Winchester to my shoulder and leveled it, the bull was turning to run, and I put a bullet through the downed log that he had been hiding behind. You have never heard a fourteen-year-old boy curse like that, especially when Dad roared with laughter. He was wise, he knew then that I

51

would remember that miss more (ahem) fondly than any actual kills I'd ever make. Well, I don't know about fondly, but it's definitely one that has provided a solid impetus in my life for bull elk redemption. This is especially true for a bull elk in the Big Hole.

Maybe it isn't exactly quiet in the timber of this country. In fact, it could be just the opposite. If you're a good listener, which is something I'm trying to improve upon in my life, you'll first hear an almost roaring whoosh of omnipresent breeze through these beautiful pines. There's also the tap-tap-taptaptaptaptap of a woodpecker or a flicker working on one of these trees. Then you might hear the peep-peep-peeppeeppeeppeep of one of those little forest birdies—one of several that you hear a lot and never see to identify it. And then there are the creaks of swaying snags, a hundred years old, maybe a gurgle of a little meandering stream.

Then I hear my dad, calling out to his oldest son, who I know is right there somewhere hunting right along with us.

Deeper and louder than the actual sounds are the memories of words spoken, and dang it, usually the words that shout out and the thoughts that bounce around in my head are those related to a negative past. It's almost as if you aren't hunting for elk at all in this country, what you're really hunting for are answers.

Why did I do what I did? Where did I go wrong in life? Why did she leave me? I have finished college, but now what do I do? There're also some more benign and neutral voices and scenes; there's Grandpa sitting in his recliner watching a ball game, many years gone now, but still saying "Ya can't eat tracks." There's Grandma, also long gone, working in the kitchen with the apron on, frying stacks of pancakes, sausage patties, and eggs for us at 3:00 in the damn morning. There's my mom telling us to be careful and good luck. There's my grandma and aunts and uncles in Helena, ready to listen to my hunting stories at Christmas. There's my buddy who *always* has good luck elk hunting, saying "I wouldn't settle for anything less than a 350-class bull." There's my beautiful wife, who tolerates all this nonsense, and my own sons, who I hope will be as into this sport as I am. And then there's the stunning reality of crashing timber and huge tan bodies and the ping of antler tines bouncing off trees as I jump yet another bull without getting a shot at him. Shit! Oh well, there's always tomorrow. I'll get a bull in this country yet, by God.

8—Unit 50

O N NUMBER HILL, ABOVE THE TOWN of Arco, Idaho, every graduating high school class since 1920 has painted its number. I can always pick out 1993, but I don't believe I've ever spotted 1920. You can do this when you're outside of Pickles Café after breakfast, toothpick in your mouth and scratching the noses on your horses as they poke through the bars of the trailer taking in all the new smells. It may be late morning, but the deer hunt opener isn't until tomorrow—you're just heading up to put in your camp—so it's pretty easy going. It may look like there's nothing for a deer to eat here, and no cover, so you wonder at first glance if this is really a good spot to hunt. "Oh well," you think to yourself, "at least we'll get some trail time for the horses," which are now barn sour from wading around in chest-high pasture grass all summer

Then you travel for a half hour or so up the Antelope Creek Road and you remember that you aren't too far away from the Frank Church—River of No Return Wilderness, one of the most wild and pristine places on the planet, and this country definitely begins to look like the mountain and forest sibling of it. Below vast and rocky peaks (you're just south of Mount Borah, Idaho's tallest) are countless timber pockets, sagebrush slopes, canyons, gulches,

55

couloirs and coulees, and all manner of geological gashes. There's water all of a sudden; there's creeks and mountain lakes. There are juniper patches and quaking aspen groves. There's no way there *couldn't* be deer. Everywhere you look it looks like the background on one of those paintings of monster mule deer bucks.

I was in the eighth grade the first time we hunted there. Even leading up to the point in the trip when I witnessed God's masterpiece of mule deer hunting country, I had told myself that this year I was going to "hold out for a big one." What this means, as a hunter, is that you'll be patient, and pass over smaller bucks in hopes you'll see a big boy to shoot. If you live by this credo, it often means that you'll end up "eating tag soup" at the end of the season, and you'll often come home skunked, without filling your freezer with deer meat.

Non-trophy hunters, non-hunters, and lots of old-timers can't understand why anyone would pass up chances, and in many instances the non-hunter will think that a hunter who comes home empty-handed a lot is not very skillful. For the hunter, it seems to be a progression of thinking, and I suppose I'm somewhere along that progression in life. With exceptions, of course, it seems to follow these stages. A young or novice hunter will put bullets in the air at the first legal game: "if it's brown, it's down." A hunter in the middle of the age or skill level of hunting, like maybe twenty to forty years old, will hold out for trophies. After you've collected a few decent specimens, you may be at the stage where I see myself now, where you wouldn't pass up, on opening day, what you would beg to see in the afternoon of the last day of the season. Then you progress to my dad's stage, where you really don't mind going home empty-handed because you're wise to the sheer amount of physical effort required after you pull the trigger. But it's an on/off switch at this stage: if you do see legal game, and it doesn't look like it's going to require Hercules to move its carcass off the mountain, you're going to shoot it.

In the eighth grade I fancied myself a trophy hunter, but I have always been able to project an image of myself, to myself, at a shallow level of consciousness, that indicates I'm a lot better at things than I really am. Deep down I have all the insecurities that anyone else does. By the time I was a ninth-grader, I hadn't really done anything remarkable as a hunter to base much confidence on, so when the sun rose over the high peaks that first morning, and a herd of does and a small forkhorn buck walked up the north side of a sagebrush slope below where I was hiking, I shot once and killed the forkhorn. Deer season had been open for about thirty minutes; so much for holding out. Grandpa would think that was awesome, and my mom would think that was awesome. My friends *might* think that was awesome. My brothers would call me an idiot. My dad just deadpanned, "Well, you got one, I guess. Good shot."

Years and years later, I took my friend Jeremy to this area. I had already killed a deer that season, so I was just along for the trip, something I love to do because there's no pressure. We packed his pickup full of gear so we could stay for a few days and try to find a good buck, but we weren't in any hurry. When we arrived at the campsite in the late afternoon, I thought I'd just take a quick look around with the binocs.

"Glassing" is a term hunters use to describe the process of looking the area over with binoculars and/or a spotting scope. It's great method for hunting because after you spot them, you can work a plan to stalk them. The rule is that you "glass close first" because you don't want to miss something near to you in favor of something far away.

I rested my elbows on the hood of Jeremy's red Chevy truck, and as you can guess, I brought the binocs up and immediately spotted a three-point buck feeding on a wide-open side hill, which we later ranged and estimated at 1,500 yards away. "Holy shit, there's one right there." I said.

Now this is good deer country, but usually you don't see them that quickly. But there he was, just having a few bites of brush and then moving a few steps, then a few more bites, then looking around. Half-joking, I asked Jeremy, "Think you could hit him from here?"

I was only half-joking because, one, it was a decent buck, two, there was no way to put a stalk on him before it got dark and, three, Jeremy is good marksman with a lot of confidence and a nice rifle (Remington Model 700, 7mm Remington Magnum). With about thirty minutes of shooting time left and a healthy dose of "fuck-it" (which Jeremy and I are both prone to), he leaned the rifle across the hood of the pickup; he got into sniper set-up and I got into spotter set-up with my Leupold spotting scope. I was prepared to witness failure. Both of us had our baseball caps turned backward and it was silent. The setting sun had created an arc of shadow on the broad face of the slope, and the deer stood right above this shadow arc in the remainder of the autumn sunshine. BANG!

The deer was so far away that there was a noticeable delay before the bullet struck home. I have never, even to this day, witnessed something shot from that far away. It seems like there may have been even a full second or two (though that's probably my mind stretching it) before I saw the deer crumple and start rolling end over end down the hill. Without optical enhancement, there was no way you could have even seen the deer, either before or after it was dead. "Well, that's that," Jeremy said with no emotion. If you were there, the next thing you'd expect him to do would be to blow the smoke from the muzzle, like a macho gunfighter on TV.

"I cannot fucking believe that!" I exclaimed. I tend to be a bit more emotional.

An hour later and the deer was in camp hanging from a tree in the coolness of the October night, and Jeremy and I were drinking beer by a campfire and replaying the brief incident. I don't recommend trying to reproduce a shot like this, as a lot of things have to come together perfectly for it to be successful. However, there is a lot about hunting that relies on fortune — and fortune must be when preparation meets opportunity. Good shot, Jeremy.

My mom is a good luck charm on hunts, and also a good cheerleader. Still, though, a hunt all by myself up through the long canyon felt a little daunting. Mom would wait in the truck for me on this hunt, as she had many times waited for us in the past as we tramped off into the darkness.

I used to sit in the truck with her when I was too little to tag along with my dad and brothers. We would listen in the silence of the truck cab for the ka-POW and the shadow echoes of rifle shots. Sometimes the little metal pings a truck makes when it cools off would sound like those shots, and we would get excited. She would always make me my own thermos of hot chocolate, and of course there were always cookies.

My dad had to travel to France during the 1990 hunting season. This left me in a quandary, as an extreme low pressure system had dumped a ton of snow around Idaho Falls, and if it snowed that much here, it must have *really* come down at Copper Basin, my deer hunting area in Unit 50. On top of that, it was late enough in the season that there would probably be bucks with any herd of does. I really wanted to go hunting, but I had never hunted alone before; and by

60

that I mean all alone, no Daddy to come to the rescue if something came up. He was on the other side of the ocean. I was fifteen years old, though, and fairly experienced in the outdoors.

My mom agreed, then, to come hunting with me the next morning. We talked it over and after considering the situation for a while, figured that we could make it work.

That night it snowed even more, the wind howling through the vents and shutters, and the snow pasting up against the windows and piling up around the trees and barn and driveway. I lay in bed wondering if I could pull this off. Soon enough though, I drifted to sleep, only to be awakened by the buzz of the alarm clock at 4:30.

We left the house at 5:00 and had the Chevy pickup in 4-high before we even got out of the driveway. Mom let me drive, knowing I had experienced these roads before, sometimes even pulling horses behind in the horse trailer. It was slow going, busting through drifts piling up on the Arco highway.

Sometime around 6:30 we turned off at Antelope Creek and headed south through the bare hills. I got out at some point and saw that the snow was over halfway up the tires on the pickup. I remember thinking, "Whoa, I better drive well and stay out of the rhubarb." The three-quarter-ton truck was brand new, though, with good tires and a powerful 350 engine; my parents must have really trusted me. Mom never said a discouraging word, she just sat bundled up in the passenger seat and looked out the window into the darkness.

We slipped, slid, crawled, and putted our way through the drifts and across the creeks and over the low hills toward the trailhead. Right before we crossed into the Salmon-Challis National Forest, we met a Chevy Blazer coming the other way; we had to go clean over in the brush so we could pass each other. The Blazer, with its wide mud tires, hopped and bounced as the driver gunned it through the deep snow. Our truck, with its brand-new pizza cutter tires, motored right through the snow. I didn't even have to rev it.

We reached the trailhead just before breaking daylight. I parked the truck facing south and west, so Mom could look over the hills with her binocs and enjoy the morning. Myself, I figured to get going so I could be in good country before shooting light, just as my dad had taught me. From my green backpack I produced a mini Mag-lite to help guide me over the trail while it was still dark. Then I shouldered the pack and my Winchester Model 70 .30-06, and with a wave to Mom, quietly clicked the truck door shut and moved off through the snow.

The morning dawned grey and cold and there wasn't any wind, but another storm was gathering. I trudged through the knee-deep snow and scanned the steep hills on either side of me. I was feeling kind of nervous as I got farther and farther from the safety of the truck, but I kept going anyhow, intent on the hunt.

About a mile up the trail, I stopped to gather myself and prepare for the shooting that could come at any time. First I took a sip of ice-cold water from my canteen. I put my Mag-lite back into my pack, tightened the sling on my rifle, inserted a 180-grain silvertip in the chamber, and put on the safety. I felt more confident now that I was ready to rock and roll.

Crossing the dry bed of the creek, I made my way through the sparse and small sagebrush over to the steep and relatively bare southeast slope to begin a climb. I play mental games with myself whenever I have to hike up a steep hill; on this day I played the game where I would go fifty steps and then stop, catch my breath, and look around. Every third time I stopped, I would exchange the rifle for my Bausch and Lomb binoculars and scan the hill above me, along with the hill across the canyon.

It was on one of my other two types of breath-catchers that I caught movement up the hill and to my right about two hundred yards off. I immediately became rigidly still until my eyes and brain came to the adrenalized conclusion that I was looking right at a mule deer doe. Very slowly I knelt down out of sight of the deer and looked down; it was time to get hold of myself and let my hunting experiences and instinct take over.

It took me about a minute to calm down and realize that I was in charge of whatever would happen next. It was time to step forward. I slid my backpack off my shoulders and laid it in the deep snow. Then I edged

63

forward on my left hip and elbow, my right hand holding the rifle.

I crawled like this until I could see the head and body of the doe; she was now joined by the heads of two more does and the front quarters and head of a 3x4 buck. I made the decision to take him.

The buck stood broadside, looking across the hill. I settled into my solid prone position, let out half a breath, and squeezed the trigger. It all had to take place that fast, or it wouldn't have taken place at all. There is not a whole lot of time for analytical thought in such situations.

In the cold air the report of the rifle seemed quick and flat, without any echo. It was followed immediately by a dull thud. The does gathered in a small bunch, trying to determine where the shot had come from. The buck slid and rolled end over end down the hill. His attempt at standing back up was met with another flat crack of rifle and another dull thud. It was all over. I would have felt bad, like I usually did when I killed an animal, but this time I was too concerned with finishing the job and making my mom and dad proud. For now, I sat and tried to get myself together and quiet the nerves, which rise to the surface of the skin and the soul after this.

After about five minutes of watching the body of the buck, which was motionless and hung up on a strong sagebrush, I stood and replaced the two spent aught-six shells from the bullet holder on my belt. I made my way in an uphill arc over to the buck—I'd been taught to always approach from the uphill side of a downed animal, in case they decide to get up and charge at you. In this case there was no danger.

Within an hour, I had the deer field dressed, the legs removed, and dragged to the bottom of the canyon. The buck carcass had slid easily downhill in the deep snow. The work really began, then, when I had to drag him over the relatively flat trail out to the truck.

Sometime in the early afternoon I caught sight of the truck and my mom caught sight of me laboring along with my kill. I will never forget the proud grin she was wearing when she met me a couple of hundred feet up the trail. We hugged and she said, "I knew you could do it." To which I responded, "It must have been your good luck, Ma!" Then I finished pulling the buck to the truck while I related the story to her just as I'd heard my dad and brothers do it.

3x4 buck because of Mom's good luck

We made it back home in the late afternoon and took some photos before I hung the deer in the barn, where I would skin him out tomorrow. All in a day's work. My dad even got to hear the news by phone that evening, and he was as proud as could be. Then right before bedtime that night my mom said, "You know, I did see a huge buck on the hill across from the truck." She has good luck.

Around seventeen, it seems like a boy kind of turns into a pseudo-superhero. Boundless energy. I was at that stage and there was no stopping me, and my mind revolved essentially around three things: football, sex, and hunting. There are, of course, minor things that accompany the big three: beer, trucks, guns, clothes, and money for dates, but those are really just tools to achieve acceptable status at the big three. I can blame my brothers for making me think about football all the time, my girlfriends for making me think about sex all the time, and the rest of my existence for thinking about hunting all the time. So I had no problem combining these when the opportunity for operating at the nexus of all three presented itself one weekend in October.

God, I love a Friday that time of year! You've got that crisp feeling in the morning, with the frost on the windshield and on the greenish/brown grass on the cleat-chewed football practice field, complemented by the orange and tan and gold aspen leaves that have fallen; they crunch when you walk on them. Your school clothes are still pretty new, you've got a steady girlfriend that you took to the homecoming dance last month, your team is undefeated and ready to make a run at the state championship, and of course, you've got two weeks left in the deer hunting season. The afternoons are dry and warm and still, the evenings smell like drifting wood smoke, and at night there are so many stars in the sky that singling out ten of them would be a daunting task.

That Friday afternoon we were boarding a bus to go play a football game in the Holt Arena on the Idaho State University campus. My mind was only one-third on football, and because this isn't a football story, I'll just tell you that we won the game. Then there was the after-game party, and because this isn't a party story, I'll just tell you that even then I could drink a bathtub full of beer and still charm a lady (at least I thought I was charming).

With every Red Solo cup of beer I chugged, and with every hour that rolled by, I would think about the fact that my dad was picking me up at 4:00 in the morning to head out to Unit 50 to hunt. Then I would remember that I am a teenaged fun-seeking super-hero, able to operate on zero sleep for days at a time. Somewhere around midnight I made the oft-repeated (in my life) decision to "fuck-it." This is not a sexual reference; it is a metaphor referring to a choice a person makes when the present is far more important than the future. If I tried to go home and get any sleep at that point, it would have been harder to wake up again than it would be if I just rolled right through the night.

At 3:00 a.m., too shit-faced to drive, I decided to walk home — which was about five miles away. Teenaged super-hero. The only thing I really remember about the walk home is stumbling over a curb in a church parking lot, and then when I caught my balance, barfing all over said parking lot. I don't remember leaving my letterman's jacket right next to the puddle of puke, but the church dude was kind enough to find my nametag on the jacket's inside flap and give me a call the next evening, telling me he had the jacket. I am often an embarrassment to my family's name.

Dad was waiting in the driveway when I walked up, but thankfully I love hunting so much that I'm usually prepared; all I needed to do was reach inside the front door and grab the three things I always have ready from September to December: rifle, backpack, and duffel bag stuffed with hunting clothes. As we drove west in the darkness, I kept having to ask Dad to pull over so I could pee. That's another cool thing about being a teenager: it seems that you metabolize alcohol quickly. But this was beginning to annoy the old man.

I especially couldn't wait to hunt this year, as I was using a brand-new Remington Model 700 BDL 7mm Remington Magnum. This was a beautiful matte-finished rifle, high-end for a working man. It had a crystal-clear Bausch & Lomb scope on it, and was sighted in to put three holes nearly on top of one another on a paper target at 100 yards.

At our spot in Unit 50, there is one long canyon that leads from the sparse flats up through scattered timber, continues through some thicker timber patches, and finally ends above the treeline just below the granite peaks. All the way up the canyon there are multiple smaller side canyons and gulches to hunt. It's mule deer hunting paradise. There are several methods for hunting deer in this kind of country. The first is the deer drive: if you have at least one hunting partner, the short straw can rustle up through the middle of the canyon making lots of noise. Any deer will likely bust out of there, either on the drive side of canyon, which makes for a sometimes challenging downhill shot, or on the other side of the canyon. You should try this only if you can make a shot across the canyon. If the canyon is too wide, you'll just end up lobbing shots like a Tony Romo football pass and either waste a bunch of ammo, or worse yet, wound an animal. But if the top of the canyon isn't more than, say, 400 yards wide, and you stay about 200 yards ahead of the short-straw guy, you'll get all kinds of opportunity.

If the deer come out on the far side, you'll have to sit down fast and compose yourself. Even though this is what you hoped for, and expected, you'll still get nervous as hell. So you quickly plop down and take a solid position with your forward wrist on your bent knee, rifle stock resting in the cupped and relaxed hand attached to this wrist. Take a couple of deep breaths now and remember that you're going to have plenty of time; even though mule deer are fast, they still have to rest as they climb the slope, especially if it's a long and steep side hill. They'll usually hop and run for a little bit, then stop and look around. If it's a big buck, sometimes he'll follow the contour of the side hill more than the does and smaller bucks will, allowing him to cover more ground. If this is the case, whistle or yell at him, and sometimes he'll stop to figure out what that noise is and where it's coming from. If he doesn't stop, just lead him a little more than you would a doe as you squeeze the trigger. Maybe put your crosshairs right on the tip of his nose.

The other way you can hunt this country is by the "rock'n'roll" method. This works if you're hunting by yourself, because instead of a driver making all the noise down in the canyon, you just find big boulders and rocks and turn them loose down your side of the canyon into the thickets below. Even if you don't scare any deer out, it's still kind of fun. One time I scared a big black bear out of the timber below me. If you don't think a bear can run fast, think again. I had a bear tag, but didn't want to blow a chance at a deer, and I might not have been able to hit that bear anyway—I'm not sure my bullets travelled that fast.

For this hunt, Dad chose to take off right up the face of an east-west ridge. I decided to walk up the main canyon for a mile or so before cutting up the long sidehill below the ridge Dad was walking on. We had planned on meeting later in the morning in a big rocky outcrop just below treeline. After a while I got bored with walking the canyon trail and decided to cut short and head straight up the slope.

The snow was deep. Backcountry skiers and snowboarders call this type of hiking "postholing," you just suck it up and work your ass off one deep snow-step at a time to get to the top of the hill. Imagine, then, doing that with a hangover and no sleep, after playing in a football game less than twelve hours before. I just played total mind games with myself. I would take three steps, then stop for thirty seconds, three more steps, stop again. I pretended I was climbing Everest, I pretended a bear was chasing my ass. I tried pretending there was a hot babe at the top of the hill and I tried pretending there was a million dollars in cash in a silver briefcase at the top of the hill. I even pretended there was a steak and a chocolate shake at the top of the hill. Finally I pretended a hot babe (topless) was at the top of the hill holding the silver briefcase in her right hand and balancing a tray with the steak and shake in her left hand. Whatever it takes, man.

The real reward at the top of the hill though, is the long rolling flat that gradually slopes up to where I was planning to meet my dad. There are three gulches in between where I was and the rendezvous point, gulches deep enough to hold deer. And I could hunt each one in succession. It was kind of like "What's behind door number one, door number two, or door number three?"

Behind door number three were about five does and a 4x4 buck—not a big one, but good enough for me (when it's good enough for you, or the average dude, you call it a "shooter"). I saw them at about the same time they saw me, about 200 yards distant. As soon as the buck separated himself from the does by walking a little bit forward, I shot him.

My shot wasn't perfect, a little too far back. The bullet made an audible thud and the buck kind of tippy-toed down the slope toward me a little, nose to the ground like a bloodhound following a track. He then stopped and arranged himself broadside to me. I had obviously pulled the shot a little. I aimed again for the firebox and squeezed the trigger. There was no audible thud this time, but when I recovered from the momentary stun of the rifle's recoil, I saw that the buck was down, and the does were trotting off.

I sat and watched for a minute to make sure the buck was down for good, and a four-shot volley of ka-bumps and ka-pows came from my dad's direction. Your hunting partner's shot in the distance has got to be one of the top-ten coolest sounds in the history of the world. I knew that my shooting had pushed some deer toward Dad, one of which I later learned was a hell of a nice 4-point. Dad got him, so now we had two deer down.

There *are* some drawbacks to hunting with a partner. Among other things, you tend to worry too much about what's up with the other guy. If he (or she) doesn't show up at the time arranged, it's disconcerting for both partners. Say I'm the guy waiting; I have to worry if everything's okay with my partner—who may be working a track or putting the final touches on a perfect stalk. He may also have an animal down, and I didn't hear the shot, and he is now field-dressing the animal, which can take awhile. These, of course, are all good things. On the other hand, and this has happened before, your partner might be in a mess somewhere. He may be lost, have a broken leg or a sprained ankle, or has had his ass kicked by a bear. Or all the above. If you're the worrying sort, the bad shit is what your mind is going to focus on, sometimes so much that you assume your hunting partner is at least dead. And if you're the hunter who's late, you worry that your partner is worrying, so if you *are* okay, you tend to walk too fast and be clumsy in order to meet that deadline, risking precisely the sort of broken-leg scene your buddy is imagining.

This wasn't exactly the case with my dad and me, but because I had heard him shoot, I wanted to see what he was shooting at, and also make it to our meeting place on time. So instead of placing some orange tape around my downed deer, or marking its location somehow (I wasn't using a GPS back then), or gutting it out and starting the drag to the truck, I just went up to the deer, made sure it was dead, and left the brand-new rifle and my pack by the deer. I figured I could follow my tracks back to it later.

After another hike to the west, I spotted my dad in the middle of a big sagebrush bowl, bent over his kill and working on it. "Hey, whadja git?" I hollered over to him.

"Pretty good 4-point," he yelled back.

"Hell yeah!"

"Was that you shooting just a minute ago?"

"Yeah, I got a decent buck too! I'll come over and help you with yours."

"Is yours taken care of yet?" he asked.

"No."

"Well, why don't you go gut yours out first."

"Okay."

Maybe I didn't mention that it had been snowing all morning. Snowing when I hiked, snowing when I shot, and snowing when I went to see what my dad had shot. And snow comes from clouds, and clouds can sock in the high country pretty quickly. Snow and socked-in clouds can cover your tracks and disorient you. It was maybe 8:00 in the morning when I shot the deer. Now it was at least 10:00 (I didn't have a watch, another mistake). The snow was falling intermittently at this point, and sometimes there were patches of sunshine (weird-ass Idaho weather), but either way, it was cold. I had not relocated the kill site, and I felt the small twinges of fatigue that come after a night of football, partying, walking, puking, and power-hiking in deep snow on steep slopes. I would see a pile of something, think it was my deer, and hike down to it. Two or three times I did this, only to have to hike back up to the elevation where I thought the deer was.

Finally, after what seemed like two more hours, I found my deer, my pack, and the rifle, all covered with a blanket of fresh snow. Now I was wet with sweat from my T-shirt all the way out to my blaze-camo jacket. I, of course, had a mullet haircut because it was the '90s, so that curly hair of mine in the back was now frozen and crunchy. Hands numb with cold, legs aching, stomach growling, and the beginnings of a headache, I went to work prepping the deer. That took an hour. Then I started dragging it.

Have you ever gone jogging with someone, or hiking or swimming, or done some kind of exercise where from the very first step you know you're in trouble? You wonder just how in the hell you are going to keep that pace or that intensity up for the entire time you're supposed to—and it's mildly terrifying. That was me and this was then. It felt like I was trying to drag a pickup truck, with its emergency brake engaged, up the hill. And I was going to have to do this for about 500 yards before I crested the ridge. Ev-er-y step was just full-on exertion. Pull and a step, pull and a step, change hand position on the rope. Don't you dare look up that hill because you know you haven't made it that far, and it's going to break your will. Keep your eyes on your feet and try as hard as you can to get that stupid song out of your head: "da-na, good thing, where have ya' gone, do do doobie do, good thing, you been gone too long," but you can keep it at bay for only a step or two before it's back and tormenting you, keeping pace with the rhythm.

But just like eating an elephant one bite at a time, or dropping one drop of water on a thousand-pound block of concrete every minute for a billion years, all that's left of the elephant is bones, and the concrete block has dissolved into dust. Far down below me I could see the pickup parked in a pullout on the main drainage road. This gave me hope and a spurt of energy, which I needed; it was now probably 1:00 or 2:00 p.m., my water bottle was empty, my fingers were stuck in the claw position, my legs were beginning to shake from fatigue, and I was running out of fuel quite quickly. "It's all downhill from here," I thought to myself.

The next part of this story should serve as a warning to always be suspicious of what looks like the "easy way out." If you took a Ruffles potato chip, put an edge of it (with the ridges pointing vertically) on a table, and then tipped it so the edge made about a sixty-degree angle with the table, that was about what I was looking down toward the truck's location. I was standing at the top of one of those side ridges; they were sparsely timbered, but had deep snow and heavy sagebrush. I started by dragging my buck right down one of those ridges. My dad had dragged his buck down an adjacent ridge, unbeknownst to me at the time, and because he is wise to the ways of topography, he stayed on his ridge until he was at the bottom. Me, I felt the pull of gravity horizontally down toward the thickly timbered gully that separated two of these ridges. I had travelled maybe a hundred yards down the ridge until the siren song of that gulley pulled me and my deer down into it. "No problem," I thought to myself, "there's a pretty good game trail right down the center of this gully."

And it was pretty easy going for another hundred yards or so. I patted myself on the back and figured it was textbook from here on down to the truck. Then I came to a log laid over the game trail. It was four or five inches in diameter, but too close to the ground to drag the deer under it, so I just had to wrestle the deer over the top of it, then take a quick breather. Another ten yards down the gully there was another similar situation. And then another and another. Add a few slick boulders in here and there, and pretty soon I found myself in a hell of a rat's-nest mess of downed timber and twigs and brush and "oh my God I am tired!"

I felt like I was in the middle of the fishing line when it gets all tangled up on your reel and you can't cast until you straighten it out, and you're doubtful you can get it straightened out, and you're thinking about just cutting off the whole mess, and you wish you had enough line to start over, and the fish are jumping like crazy and it's a near emergency. I began to get that panicky feeling because I knew my dad was probably waiting for me by now, and I didn't want to make him worry. There was just no way I could go any faster, even though my mind kept telling me, "You better get moving, boy!"

The more I tried to hurry, the slower it seemed I could go and the less progress I made. This was like lifting weights while simultaneously competing in a 10K road race. The day was waning and late afternoon was coming on hard. I was operating on no food or water, just the remnants of teenage energy, and the knowledge that it seemed to be either sink or swim. It never occurred to me to just frickin' bag it, hike down to the truck, get some water and food, and make another assault on it later. That's the conundrum of having all that teenage energy but lacking the brains and experience to make good choices in applying it.

So I kept at it. At this point, I didn't dare stop because I knew I would cramp up and that would be it. My backpack and clothes at this point were a bloody, sopping wet, muddy mass. Unfortunately, so was the brand new rifle, though I could hardly care. I had even dropped it once, so there was dirt down the barrel. Both lenses on the scope were caked with muddy ice. I started to get a feeling of mild hysteria, and lashed out at the woods and the deer and the world a couple of times. "God-DAMMIT!!" I would yell. "Fuck hunting, fuck this shit forever!" I shed tears of frustration and fatigue. That's about when I made it to the bottom of the hill and had just 200 yards of flat pulling left, with no game trail and even more choking off by downed logs and saplings. Now I was even encountering willows. A rain/snow mix fell steadily and the afternoon chugged on to early evening. Finally I yelled in frustration one last time and just plopped down in the snow/mud. The deer at this point barely even looked like a deer anymore, just a ball of mud.

I don't admit to thinking of my dad as a hero very often. I don't because for some reason I feel like it might make me less of a man, which I realize is dumb, but that's just how it is. But I cannot dispute the fact that for the dozen or two times in my life that I have *really* been behind the 8-ball, he has appeared out of nowhere. There's a common metaphor for his style, though, and that's of the father who goes out in a boat to rescue his drowning son by pulling up alongside him in the boat and reaching out with the paddle for the son to grab hold of. Before the dad will let the kid grab onto the paddle though, the dad gives the son a few whacks over the top of the head with it, I guess to teach a lesson; that's kind of been my old man's style. But my God did I feel delivered when I saw him working his way up through that willow deadfall shithole to rescue me.

"What the hell are you doing in here?" he asked. "That rifle is all fucked up now. Whose rifle is that, anyway? You should have stayed on the ridge. That's all you had to do. I just took my deer down on the next ridge over and the damn thing basically slid right down to the truck on its own."

While I sat crossed-legged in the mud with my lower lip pooched out and the look of a defeated little bitch on my face, he grabbed the rope and hauled that dead mess of hide and bone and muscle and mud the rest of the way through the rat's nest and across the creek and flung it into the back of the pickup. Teenage boys cross back and forth from being all bad-ass to being just silly little turds. I started the day as the former, and ended squarely at the latter.

"Wow," he said, "whoever owns that rifle, they're going to be pissed off at you when you bring it back. You should've just stayed on the ridge."

I was indeed pretty pissed at myself.

It doesn't take long to run out of money at college. Especially when you're a dickhead like me and you operate on a champagne lifestyle with your income more like a beer budget. I had to sell that rifle within a few weeks of starting college at the University of Idaho in Moscow. That deer hunt was the last time I hunted with the rifle, and the last time I hunted in Unit 50 for another twelve years. The dill-hole I sold it to shot what was the state record whitetail at that time, exactly one Saturday after the transaction. The buck was standing in a farmer's field and the guy was delivering papers in his Geo Metro. As cool as that rifle was, it had some sort of bad juju for me.

9—Northern Idaho

I WAS PRETTY SURE I HAD MADE the best decision of my young adult life when I drove south from Coeur d'Alene toward Moscow in August 1994. Never mind what would happen at the University of Idaho — yeah, yeah, I'd go to class, do some homework, blah, blah. First priority, though, had to be hunting. Now *this* looked to be the true sportsman's paradise — timber patch here, open field there, creek here, lake there, mountain over there, brushy side hill ahead. Whitetails and elk, rifles and packs, hike-hike and boom-boom!

Oh, how good it is to be able to put everything you own in the back of a pickup. That's how my brother Tom and I lived, and the only regret I have now is that I didn't enjoy it more. There is world-class whitetail deer hunting within minutes of downtown Moscow, Idaho, and to hear the average jackass describe it, it's like shooting fish in a barrel. Boy, did I buy into that lock, stock and barrel — so much so that I changed my major before the first semester was even finished. I changed from pre-med (yeah, who wants to be a doctor and makes loads of money) to wildlife biology, simply because I planned on becoming the world's greatest hunter, and as I viewed it, this degree I was now seeking was essentially a hunting degree.

Let me be clear, however, that it's a hunting degree simply because the classes are harder than they should be, and you don't study as hard as you should, so you get lousy grades, get depressed, and choose to spend most of your time hunting. There is not a single class about big-game hunting, but by my third semester at U of Idaho, I was becoming damned experienced at pursuing northern Idaho big game because I went deer and/or elk hunting every single day of the season.

A couple of other things I learned about this country: 1) it's not as simple to connect as everyone made it sound, mainly because the only easy elk and whitetailed deer are on private land, which I found extremely hard to get access to, and 2) it rains a lot, and 3) the ghosts and frustrations of grades and life follow you around in that thick timber.

But I must remind myself that I'm a "possibilities person" and I live for the chance that something cool might happen. So I was all open to awesome possibilities when Tom took me out after whitetails on the opening day. We went to a place we later started calling Deer Road.

It *is* true there's an excellent population of whitetailed deer in these north Idaho units, but the best chance you have to get one is on private land. These huge grainfields with mosaic patches of timber are like the country you see on the Outdoor Channel's whitetail hunting programs. The idea here is that you put up tree stands in areas where you've seen deer feeding, or along game trails where your motion-sensor trail camera has picked up deer moving through in the early mornings and late evenings. I suppose bowhunting would work well here, too, but I haven't really gotten into archery yet.

So Tom and I did what most American hunters do, and that's to go enjoy access to the land we all own, be it through the state Department of Lands, or on Forest Service or Bureau of Land Management land. Deer Road was state land, and you park your truck at a concrete Jersey barrier set up to permanently block motor vehicle access, and you start walking down Deer Road. I can almost guarantee you that even though you're trying your damnedest to be quiet, you'll make a tiny cough, or clear your throat, or crack one little twig and then you hear a sudden snort and see at least three white "flags" shoot up and bound away from you into the thickest timber you'll ever hunt in. Those flags are the white tails of the whitetailed deer you just jumped, and they act as a warning signal to all the other deer, telling them to "light the pipes, here comes a redneck!"

You whisper "goddammit" to yourself and continue on down the logging road because you read or heard somewhere (but never in any of the college classes you've taken) that whitetails will sometimes circle around rather than just bug out like an elk would.

This logging road that we walked down was like the main vein into the heart of the hunting spot. It bordered a huge park-like meadow with a nice willowy stream running down the center of it. I suppose that when it's high summer you'd see deer out there after daylight, but whitetails, I learned, are damn smart animals, and I never saw a single one in that meadow in the six years I hunted Deer Road. It didn't keep me from focusing way too much of my visual attention out there, though.

When there was snow on the ground, the numbers of deer tracks in this country were amazing. They crisscrossed everywhere on the road and led off into the timber. At first I assumed you could track these bastards like you would an elk in the Big Hole Valley, and time after time after time I would just scare up white flags and snorts. It took me a long time to learn this lesson. I had also nearly forgotten the powerful effect of a still and silent world on the booming and blaring hyperactivity of my mind and emotions.

This could be why I missed so many chances at these deer, because I would often get lost in my thoughts after I ducked into the timber after a track that seemed bigger than the others. The track rarely moseyed and meandered; instead it usually took off like a bee-line.

It's hard still to reconcile and figure out my time and my purpose for ever being at the University of Idaho. It may go down in my personal history as the biggest failure of my life on a medium scale, as in academics and economics, but then as I ponder it now on a broader scale, it may have been a collection of the greatest life lessons I will ever experience. It may have been my lottery of learning.

I would start down Deer Road each morning with an expensive and properly-stocked backpack, the best hunting clothes and boots you could buy at the time, and a perfectly okay rifle. I started each pre-dawn morning with a clean attitude and with my eternally optimistic expectation that this would be the day I would score. I think this latter thing is crucial to all hunters. Once you lose that expectation that you're going to get some action, you'd better just quit for the day, or quit forever, because that's when you're going to jump him — the Boone and Crockett buck or bull that you've seen only in paintings until now. Or maybe it'll just be a shooter. Either way, it's got to be the driving force behind it, especially for some mornings on Deer Road when the rain is steadily falling and it's doing the "depression drizzle" out there, and Deer Road is a muddy mess, and your scope and binocular lenses are all wet and foggy, and the rain is turning to snow now and then, but then it turns back into rain, then it turns into something that isn't even snow or rain or sleet, it's like sneet, or reet, or slow, but it's a mixture of all things that are wet and cloudy and foggy and cold. Yet you still try to look on the bright side and say to yourself "well, it'll be easy to be quiet."

Then you dive into what I can best describe as a forest from something J.R.R. Tolkien wrote about. To someone with less imagination, or translated, someone who doesn't have mental issues, this forest is simply a thick collection of *Pseudotsuga menziesii* (Douglas fir), *Pinus contorta* (lodgepole pine), and a few *Larix occidentalis/laricina*(Western larch/Tamarack). To me, those trees were a physical metaphor for the hiding places of the spooks and trolls and goblins in my brain.

Behind some of the trees I would feel like a failure for dropping half my credits at college this semester, with a report card that looked like this: W W C- C- (Withdraw, Withdraw, C minus, C minus). Behind other trees there was my bank account statement, which looked like this: Current Balance $-157.53, and a credit card statement that looked like this: Current Balance $10,762. But those are common demons. Murkier and more insidious were the thoughts that revolved around my failures at controlling alcohol consumption and — even deeper than that — the specter of many failed relationships (romantic, platonic, familial, and friendly) and the growing ice ball of mental disorder. Finally, there was my consistent failure to locate and kill the subject of this story, the goddamn whitetailed deer.

The season and my tag were open for either sex, because the population was strong, but I doubt I would have ever even gotten a shot at a doe or a fawn using my current tracking method. You can see from the last paragraph how my thoughts can wander when I tracked, so it's no surprise that when I was in the deepest recesses of my mental Mirkwood Forest, I would be quickly brought back to reality by a literal bucksnort and at least three white flags running away from me.

I happened to be watching TV one evening after a day of hunting, enjoying the *Buckmasters* program on a sports channel. They were slaying bucks left and right on this program, whitetails and muleys, and when they revealed that they were hunting near Peck, a small town north of Lewiston, I packed my gear and got ready to leave the very next morning.

I guess I'd had it with hunting the thick timber of the Deer Road area near Bovill, and I was tired of snorts and white flags and fruitless tracking. Truthfully, even to this day, I prefer to hunt in areas with deep canyons and high mountains. I like to sit and glass for animals. I could do it all day long. My dad and my brother, I think, prefer to dive into that thick timber, and I can do that too, of course, but I *prefer* wide open spaces.

Within twelve hours I was sitting on a rim of a deep canyon looking at four different groups of deer. The closest bunch were all whitetails, the rest were mule deer. I was okay with that, I hadn't bagged a flag (whitetail) yet, but I was getting a little bloodthirsty, so a muley would suit me fine.

One thing I noticed about a lot of the country in northern Idaho was a kind of "inversion" in the topographical way you hunt. In the southeast part of Idaho, and southwest Montana, where I had done all my previous hunting, you start out at the bottom, i.e. that's where you park your truck, and the mountains and canyons and all the rest of the macro-geological features are above you. In that country, you generally hike uphill to get your game, and then you drag it back downhill to the truck. Here in the Highway 12 corridor (and actually in the more open parts near

Kendrick and Deary), you start on top and you're always looking *down* into a canyon, rather than *up* at a ridgetop. I don't really know how to explain this, or if maybe it was just those particular areas where I was sniffing around, but I'll say this, it never did occur to me that if you shot something, you were going to be hauling its dead ass back *up* the hill, not down. Gravity would be your mortal enemy.

The first day in that country was more of a scouting trip; the next week, however, I got down to biznatch. I took my old high school buddy Bryce with me, who was now going to college up here. I have had very few hunting partners outside of my family; there are pros and cons of hunting with other people—especially people who aren't family. A couple of things about Bryce, though: first, he is almost family, as I've known him since I was in elementary school; second, he loves hunting, is always prepared, and pays his half of fuel and food and stuff; and third, no matter how tough it gets, he will never ever give up. This third thing can be literally a lifesaver in the big country where we hunt. If you're a pansy, this big country can kill you. At the very least, if you can't hack working in the freezing cold or the baking heat, on steep hills, through muddy and snowy bottoms and jungle timber, all the while packing at least the weight of a rifle and backpack, you'll be forcing your hunting buddy to work harder than he should have to, and Daddy ain't always gonna be there to bail you out.

One of the coolest things about taking off in the early morning hours for hunting is coffee; and at the time, Copenhagen. Oh, and Dire Straits. With the hugest mug of coffee you can buy (it was 32 oz. then, now you can buy those ridiculous "big-buddy" mugs that contain like a keg of coffee) on the seat next to me, I would wait until I hit the city limits and then turn on the power to my Chevy truck's tape deck. All hunting season, the only tape that was allowed in there was Dire Straits' *On the Night*, their '93 live album. Then I would take my first scalding sip of black coffee and stuff a big dip of Copenhagen into the left side of my upper lip as "Calling Elvis" was sneaking into the speakers via brushes on the snare drum. There are so many myths about Elvis that I started thinking of whitetail bucks as Elvis—I'd had many Elvis sightings, but I could never determine whether they were my imagination or the real thing. Damn whitetails.

It took about two and a quarter turns through the entire *On the Night* tape to get to my Peck hunting spot—so that would mean "Walk of Life" was reaching the pedal steel solo by Paul Franklin at about the time we pulled into the pull-off spot. It's a strange sensation, then, when you shut off the truck because you have to go from rock'n'roll played fairly loud to what should be utter silence. You can't even shut the doors normally on the truck—you have to keep your hand on it until it makes contact with the doorframe on the truck's body, and then just push on it until it clicks shut. And for God's sake, don't ever use your keyless to lock it so that the horn toots. Sound carries forever on cold mornings. But you also have to plan on some immediate exertion, and in much colder temperatures than what you were just experiencing inside the softness of the pickup. In short, it's like being born.

At the barbed wire fence across the road, I held Bryce's rifle while simultaneously stepping on the lower strands of the fence and pulling up on the upper strands to create an opening for him to slide through. He did the same for me. All Western kids learn this technique at about age six, when you become too big to fit through the strands on your own. The rifle holding part you learn later in hunter safety class, if your dad or grandpa hasn't already taught you.

The sun was just barely starting some orange-ish color in the east. On all accounts, it looked like it was going to be a beautiful day.

As we picked softly through the brush on the rim of the canyon, my eyes continued to attempt to adjust to the terrain. Even when it's basically full-on dark, you are still trying to figure out whether you can see animals, and your eyes begin to make you believe you are seeing animals. I hoped Bryce wouldn't start thinking I was a nice buck, or worse yet, a bear; the guy *is* pretty excitable, and he's terrified of bears.

After a while we stood in the stillness on the canyon rim to collect our thoughts, and maybe just to enjoy being alive and having an opportunity like this. I was about to whisper something to him when I heard what kind of sounded like the scrape of shale and some footsteps in the hard earth at a distance. We spoke in the hunter's whisper.

"You hear that?"

"Yeah. Whaddaya think it is?"

"I'm not sure, but I bet it's deer. I was gonna suggest we go on down a little farther, but maybe we oughta hang here for a minute until we can see what that is."

So we sat quietly down and pulled out the binocs (or as a lot of hunters call them, the glasses). They gather a lot more light than the naked eye, so it didn't take long for us to pick out the deer that were making those little crunches and scrapes, *about 300 yards away from us* across this first canyon. This is what I meant when I said that sound carries a long ways on mornings like this!

Now we were basically pinned down; if we spooked these deer, they would likely bug out to the next canyon, or the next one after that, and thereby alert all the deer that might be hanging out in those canyons. We sat side by side and got watery eyes from peeling them back through the eyepiece lenses of our binocs, and runny noses from the morning chill and the light up-the-canyon breeze (this anabatic/katabatic wind combination is like the life of an old man—goes up in the morning, goes down at night). We could see the basic shapes and silhouettes of the deer, but couldn't make out genders or antlers yet. They just fed right on out in the open along the east wall of the canyon.

The other predicament this presented us was that hunting season had been open for a while, so any good bucks would likely split off from the herd not long after shooting light (sometime around a quarter to seven this time of year); they don't get big by hanging out on open side hills at daylight during the season — or as many a hunter has said, "They don't get big and old by being stupid." So we just strained our eyes harder as the deer fed down and away from us.

After what seemed like maybe an hour, we just could not make out any antlers, so we stood back up and moved quietly east along the rim, a disked grain field down on our left, bordered by some tall grass and a broken century-old fence; the deep deer canyon system ranged off to our right. The plan was to just continue on this rim and possibly roll some rocks down into the ravines. It's good to hunt with someone you know, someone who knows what to do. We didn't need to discuss much — it's all understood, so we could just move silently along as the sun continued to glide into the morning, watching left, right, in front and in back of us for any deer. It is so very interesting how your senses become almost prehistoric in these situations, like you're a damn caveman; only instead of a spear, you're packing a thunderstick.

If you don't have any introspection capability, or the desire to daydream, I suppose this part of hunting can get a little boring. For me, seeing the wide-open spaces was a refreshing change from the jungle I'd been hunting for the past couple seasons. I also like to poke along and daydream about what I'd do if I won the lottery, or which guns I want to buy. I can usually avoid the more sinister thoughts in the wide-open country, though occasionally I have to force myself to avoid thinking that what I really should be doing right now is sitting in class or doing homework. But the sport at this point does require persistence, because the next three canyons seemed to hold no deer, even after we rolled a half-dozen big rocks, crashing down the slope from our vantage point.

Now it was late afternoon and I was about to apologize to Bryce for insisting he skip work and school to come down here with me, and he wasn't seeing as many deer as I had promised. "Tell you what," I said, "I'm gonna hang here and glass those canyons farther south from here. I don't care if you keep going and check that next canyon. It looks pretty bare, though; not much cover to hide a deer."

Moments later, from the corner of my eye I picked up a frantic motion waving for me to "get the hell over here."

Did you ever watch the TV show M.A.S.H., when the opening music is played and it shows everyone running out to the helicopters and they have to bend over low to avoid being struck by the chopper blades? I call that the "hunter run" because, though you always try to avoid running while hunting, especially since you're carrying a loaded rifle, you always feel like you have to run in kind of a crouch, bending over at the waist. That's how I covered the 50 or so yards to Bryce's position, like I was ducking rotor blades, to see why he was beckoning me. I knew it wasn't because he wanted to make small talk.

"Check it out, dude! There's a huge fuckin' buck bedded right on the open sidehill!" He wasn't screaming audibly, it was that excited hunter hiss-whisper. It's the predator-hushed equivalent of yelling.

At first I couldn't see anything. The open side of the canyon facing us seemed as bare as a baby's butt. And gray. This was October, and with no snow cover, all the vegetation was more or less dormant, void of all color except gray and maybe tan. But eventually with the binocs I picked out the buck lying broadside to us, maybe 250 yards away. It appeared to be fast asleep. It may be that because I was so focused on harvesting a whitetailed buck, I declared to Bryce that that is exactly what the deer was. He disagreed. "That's a mule deer. Are you stupid?"

It didn't matter either way because this management unit was open for both species. Besides that, how cool is it that we were in country where there was opportunity for either one? It is biologically true that the two species can interbreed, though it isn't common. As I understand it, it will usually be a whitetail buck with muley does, not the other way around. The crosses typically happen where preferred habitat overlaps; the mule deer favor certain habitats and elevation and the whitetails other areas, and at the edges you will sometimes see these hybrids.

Hunter etiquette dictates that he (or she) who sees first gets to shoot first, all else being equal. In this situation, I actually told Bryce I didn't plan on shooting at all—and to know Bryce is to know that his response was probably something like, "Don't worry about it, you're not gonna get the chance anyway, I'm going to kill it with one shot."

So we both lay down on our bellies and got into shooting position. Bryce opened up with his Remington Model 600 "Mohawk" 6mm Remington. This is a neat little compact rifle that works well for women and kids and thick timber. Cross-canyon shots are not the specialty of this type of rifle. Boom-kapowecho!! Boom-echo!! That buck was awake now! Bryce's shots had kicked up a couple poofs of dust and that acted as the starting gun for an Olympic sprint. That was no damn whitetail, it was a nice mule deer buck. Don't look for them to run back uphill and have to stop every twenty-five yards and look around like a doe or fawn or a young buck. He was using gravity in his favor—heading straight downhill and moving out! Bryce was three or four shots into this when I just could not stand it anymore, so I blew off the front right leg of the sprinting buck—not on purpose, but it slowed it down for Bryce to make some kind of connection with the remaining shells in his rifle. Then he was out of bullets and the buck was at the bottom of the hill, still working hard to bug out. I had four shells left. "You want me to take him, dude?" I asked.

Without waiting for, or hearing, a response, I made a hasty shot and heard and saw what I knew was the end of the hindquarters on that deer. When you put a 180-grain .30-06 bullet into the back end of a big game animal, it sounds like you're whipping a huge flyswatter against the wall of your kitchen. Thwaaackkk!!! If there's one redeeming result of this accident, it's that the animal is not going anywhere now (I'm always trying to make lemonade from lemons). It isn't something to be proud of, because I'm sure it causes indescribable misery, and the best you'll get out of the hindquarters now is maybe ten pounds of hamburger. "Good shot," Bryce deadpanned.

It seems like a lot of people deadpan flippant remarks to me after I shoot.

Then I had to do the final act and put a last bullet just behind the ears of the 6x7 mule deer buck, ending its misery and beginning ours. It was only after that last shot that I recalled that the topography is inverted here in northern Idaho, and I was not experienced enough at hunting this country to take that into consideration when we'd started blasting away. That deer was not going to be dragged downhill to a waiting pickup. That deer was 200 yards below us in a canyon steep enough that even sliding down would be challenging. Hiking up a hill this steep, even if you weren't carrying any extra weight, would require that you use all fours. Oh boy.

After pictures and high-fives and field dressing, we hooked a rope around the buck's antlers and each grabbed a base angle of the loose triangle it made with that attachment. "Okay, here we go," I said, as if it were going to be just some mild everyday exertion.

And we made it maybe five feet before I knew we were screwed. It was so steep that our boots just basically peeled out in the soft dirt. We both sounded like freight trains as we tried to catch our breath. "This just ain't gonna work," I declared.

At least at this point in my life I had begun to recognize times when I get in over my head. It had taken nearly twenty years for me to learn how to determine that, and this situation was turning out to be one of those lessons along that path. We ended up doing some butchering right there in the field.

The buck Bryce and I killed below
the ridge and then had to pack back up!

Most people consider the two long straps of muscle that run along each side of an ungulate's backbone as the best meat — it's referred to as the backstrap, also known as filet mignon when cut into little steaks. There are the top two, which I loosely call sirloins, and the bottom two, inside the body cavity, which are properly called tenderloins. Thankfully, these weren't bloodshot from our poor marksmanship, so we skinned back the buck's hide to expose these cuts; we removed them and tucked them into a plastic bag.

97

Then you have four quarters consisting of the two front shoulders and the two larger hindquarters.

Because the right-hand hindquarter was hammered, I just cut it off with my Buck knife and Gerber saw and left it for the coyotes. This situation called for some *phronesis*, as I was not going to pack out a bunch of bloodshot ribbons of gristle just to throw them away at home. We were left with three decent quarters, and because Bryce was considering some taxidermy on this deer, we also had a cape, head, and antlers to pack out. All told, gear included, we had easily in excess of two hundred pounds of stuff to haul up the hill and then about two miles across the flats back to the pickup. It was going to be a long afternoon, and we had only one quart of water for the two of us. You'd think I would have learned my lesson from my last mule deer hunt down in Unit 50.

When we got home late that night, I tried to turn on the kitchen faucet to wash my hands and get a drink. All that came out was a momentary hiss of air. Evidently the toilet had been leaking and it had run my whole water well's holding tank dry. Bryce was staying with me at the time, so he was screwed too. We just drank what was left of our Keystone Light and fell asleep bloody, tired and sore.

At the time, I was living in a trailer fifteen miles east of Moscow, just below Moscow Mountain. Living out in the woods, it should have been no surprise to me when a black bear dragged away the head and antlers of the deer in the night. We could see its tracks the next morning in the dust in the shed where we had tossed everything. Thankfully, though, we found what was left of it a few days later down the slope a ways. I hope Bryce still has that rack, and if he does, I ought to go look at it each time before I go hunting, to remind me that the real work starts when you pull the trigger — just like Gramps always said.

So maybe I had been part of a successful mule deer hunt, but the ghostly whitetail still eluded me — and this seemed to call for for desperate measures. I started the fall semester of 1996 with sixteen credits of classes, but was forced to reduce that to four credits in order to pursue the more important endeavor of bagging Elvis.

I started the '96 season off in dubious fashion, missing four cross-canyon shots at a spike bull elk, and this apparently pushed a bull elk to every other hunter in the canyon below Freezeout Ridge that morning. When I drove home that afternoon, it seemed like there was an elk hanging in every camp.

To this day, even though I preach and try to live for "just getting out there," I still get bloodthirsty and envious when I see antlers and legs hanging in garages or camps, or spilling out the backs of pickups. In fact, it's the only time of year that if I'm driving down the interstate I'll look harder at the backs of trucks to see dead animals then I will at the passenger compartments of cars to see pretty girls.

And then my brother Tom nailed a really nice whitetail buck on Deer Road. This is the same Tom who was beginning to preach his growing lack of enthusiasm for hunting, the same Tom who had never even purchased his own hunting rifle—he'd just annexed my dad's Remington Model 760 when he moved to Moscow. This is the same Tom who, on a hunt at Deer Road just a couple of weeks before, had gotten angry *at the rain* and fired two .30-06 rounds into the sky in an attempt to kill it. But this was also the same Tom who was, by training, a deadly hunter and marksman—never mind which rifle he used or what he was shooting at. It should have come as no surprise that he'd get Elvis-the-Whitetail first.

The big buck had stepped out from hiding in the thick timber onto one of the numerous overgrown log-skidding trails that crisscrossed the area. At about twenty-five yards, his first shot was through the firebox, and the deer just stood there for a moment. Tom's second 180-grain silvertip behind the shoulder dropped the buck to the ground. The shoulder mount of it is still in my dad's basement, along with all the other deer and elk that look as though they plowed through the drywall and got stuck there on the wall.

Instead of draining my enthusiasm, though, this caused me to hunt even harder. I was happy for Tom, but still in need of my own sense of closure. And on the second-to-last day of the season, I got it—because I learned that though it may not be possible for me to sneak up on a whitetailed deer, with patience the deer might come to me.

If there are two months that are twins of each other in Idaho, they are February and November. In fact, there have been times when I've been driving home during either of the months and it suddenly escapes me, and I have to actually ask myself, "Is it almost winter? Or almost spring?" If it's almost winter, that means the grand finale of the year is just about here, which is the last day of hunting season, and which is marked and celebrated traditionally through Thanksgiving week (for me at least). If it's almost spring, that means I'm getting cabin fever and getting sick of wading through mud and muck to feed chickens, and getting sick of gray days, and getting sick of trying to decide whether or not I need to lock in the hubs of my truck.

But in 1996 I had no doubt in my mind that it was nearing the end of November. Although the deer season in Unit 8 was open into the first week of December, this would have to be my last week, because I was going to go back to Idaho Falls, ostensibly to enjoy Thanksgiving with my parents, but truthfully just to drink beer with my friends Cory and Paul. This would have to be it; this was going to be my last chance at my own Elvis.

I had hunted so many times that year I could almost prep all my gear, drive to Deer Road, and walk into the hunting area blindfolded, which actually wasn't too far from the truth that morning. The snow was falling straight down in the headlights — the lazy, heavy flakes that you know are just adding layers to snow already on the ground. My 1993 Chevy truck did not have lock-out hubs like my "new" 1995 Toyota does, so when I started climbing the little hill outside of Moscow, all I needed to do was jerk the transfer case lever back into 4-HI when the highway started getting slick. I could feel the front-differential engage and the tires grip the road, and I heard the "thunk." There was a little indicator light down by the lever and instead of having just the two rear tire icons light up, all four were now orange. I sped up to 60 and Mark Knopfler began his raspy singing. I put in the dip, took a sip of hot black coffee, and thought about what it means to hunt solo.

Times had changed for me. Times had changed for hunting, or maybe it was just the area I hunted now. It seems like the only similarity between the nature of my hunting now, and that of the Montana Mule Deer 1980s hunts, was the fact that I had coffee and a rifle. Yeah, I hunted with Tom now and then, but he had never really had the passion for it that I did. I still went hunting with my dad when we drew late cow-elk tags, but he didn't like to hunt whitetails (because they kicked his ass too, though he'll never admit it), Stan was gone, and Gramps was too old to go now — so solo was about the best or maybe only way for me.

This continual coming home empty-handed was beginning to have some effect on me. At first it was seriously annoying — especially because I saw so many deer and never got a shot. It was like a video game that you have no idea how to play, so you lose all three lives immediately, every time — or a game of chess with a smart-ass pro who pulls a checkmate on you in just four moves. And does it more than twice. Other people were getting whitetails, so I was like, what the hell? I'm not going to say that I had quenched my bloodthirst, I just think I had buried it somehow, meaning even though I was still *hoping* to kill a deer, I no longer *expected* it. Today I was not going to track whitetails or walk around and look for whitetails. Today I planned on marching through the darkness of that haunted forest around Deer Road right onto a little bump in the topography that I knew was at the end of one of the branching skid trails. I would find a tree, sit with my back against it, and not allow myself more than twenty total movements, other than the rising and falling of my breathing, from sunup until sundown. For me, this was some grand epiphany, to sit there all Zen-like and contemplate the goings-on while using the deer's own movements and habits against him, rather than mine against me. For most people, this is simply called still-hunting, or stand-hunting. I was in sniper mode.

I could not have a picked a worse weather-day to do this, but I had made up my mind. Not long after sunup, the snow turned to softly falling rain, which became sleet, and then, almost as if Mom Nature had decided "fuck-it," the sleet just turned to rain. I sat quietly as the rain came down, sometimes as mini-bombs, sometimes in sheets, but mostly as the depression drizzle. When I had first sat back against the tree, there was at least a foot of snow on the ground, but as the day wore on the snow became slush, which then just became a mess. And I waited.

And I waited more. I may have stood two or three times to pee, but other than that I just sat and tried to make sure the lenses on my scope stayed dry. At one point, I sat forward to ease my aching back, and a river of water travelled through some previously unknown space between my coat and pants and straight down my butt crack. This was the most miserable day I had had hunting up to this point in my life, but by two or three in the afternoon, I had come so far that I figured I might as well see it on through.

Whitetail bucks make a sound that I can best describe as a burp. It's technically called a "grunt," and it's something they generally will do during the rut. Dirty bastards. But really it's just like "baaahp." What happened next came so fast that there was no prelude (other than the three previous hunting seasons that had led up to this moment). Just before I was going to give up on whitetails for good and forever, it was getting dark enough that things were starting to lose their color. *Baaahp.* Here came a whitetail buck and two does with the afterburners on, headed right past me at about thirty yards.

I don't know what he was burping about, but I knew they were movin' out. I tried to pick a clearing in the timber to make the shot. No way. I tried to follow him in the scope. No way. No way was I not at least gonna pull the trigger, though.

POW! I wasn't shooting at anything; I couldn't even see him in the scope. I was just making a point. It was actually somewhat startling to hear my rifle go off in this country, as I had carried it cold and fully loaded for nearly three seasons now without ever once cutting loose.

Anyone who's been shooting or hunting with me knows I can work a bolt on a bolt-action rifle damn near as fast as a semi-automatic (which isn't bragging, it's actually not something to be proud of), so I was ready when that buck made his fatal mistake and the whitetail hunting gods finally threw me a bone. For some reason, he made a ninety-degree turn to the left and ran right at me!

This was all happening so fast that I really couldn't figure out what to do. The buck was coming hard and again I couldn't pick him up in my scope in this low light — and at such a close distance. When he got to, no shit, about five yards, he finally saw me and turned another ninety degrees, on a dime, to his right. I simply held my .30-06 at arm's length and pulled the trigger. It was so dark by then that the muzzle flash blinded me for a second, but I was sure I'd seen a tuft of hair floating down, and I knew there was no way I could have missed. Start to finish, this scene probably took place over a span of three or four seconds.

I had to sit for a moment and try to process what had just happened. "I got him. I think I got him. I think I got the motherfucker." It was like the coyote finally *catching* the roadrunner.

It was getting dark. Fast. I tried to follow his tracks in the slush and mud, but it was no use. A flashlight wasn't even helping. And of course, when I told Tom and Bryce about it that night, when I came home empty-handed, they listened with the syrup of skepticism.

The next day, though, I did convince Tom and his buddy Dave to accompany me back to the scene of the crime, as if they were a couple of detectives wanting to solidify their hunches that I was nothing but full of shit.

The depression drizzle had continued on through the night and wasn't letting up as we retraced my steps back to the tree I had sat against (and brilliantly marked with a bouquet of orange surveyor's tape). God, what a muddy mess. We fanned out from the tree and started poking through the metaphorical haystack for any sign of a downed whitetail buck, and it wasn't long before Tom found him, and it wasn't hard to find Tom, gagging and hollering at me through the trees.

"Blaaagh! I fou- Blaaaghh! I found- Blaaagh! Blaaaagh! I Blaaaaaagh! Fuck, he's over here dude! Blaaaaagh!"

"What the hell's the matter?" I yelled back.

"You fuckin' gut-shot him, dude, and it's fuckin' disgusting!"

I could also hear Dave laughing.

Well, it was pretty gross; not my best work. The buck had made it only about fifty yards past where I had put a 180-grainer through his food processing equipment, which now flowered out both sides of his body through gaping entrance and exit wounds. Looking at the bright side of things, the bullet had done much of the field dressing work. The even brighter side was that I had finally gotten my damn whitetail buck, and I didn't care that Dave and Tom and I had one miserable muddy chore to drag it back to the truck.

It would be best if the story ended there, but unfortunately, as in Montezuma's Revenge, there was a vengeance that the whitetail buck exacted on me.

The meat on that deer smelled funky the whole time I was butchering it. Well, first, we have always hung our game animals for a certain period of time to let the meat age. What I never realized is that temperature is the key factor there. If you're gonna let a carcass age for better flavor and tenderness, it's got to be done under controlled conditions, like in a meat cooler, or in the barn in November where the temperature stays above freezing, but below about 40°F. My whitetail buck stayed in a shed for at least a northern Idaho November week, which saw temperatures fluctuate between 20° and 50°F. Second, being an idiotic broke college kid, I simply cut meat off the bone in no particular fashion when I butchered it, and then put those odd cuts in ruggedly wrapped butcher paper (without first putting the cuts inside plastic wrap) and sealed them with black electrical tape because I was either too broke or too lazy to go buy masking tape. One package of meat, I recall, had the words "Whitetail Ass Roast" written on it in green magic marker.

The first time I unwrapped one to cook, it stank so badly that I had to drink twelve Bud Lights before I could even begin to work on it. This was contrary to what I'd understood previously about whitetail deer meat, which was that it was supposedly really clean and good to eat. I called Tom and asked him about it. His response, "Well, you gut-shot that thing, or don't you remember? That meat's probably rotten, but you killed it, so you've got to eat it. If you just put vinegar on it every time before you cook it, it'll be fine."

So each time I cooked whitetail, which was nearly every night, due to the obvious college-kid financial situation, I would marinate the meat in vinegar for an hour before throwing it the frying pan and cooking it until it was rock hard (another of my brother's dubious culinary suggestions for rotten deer meat). The only other things I ate that winter were Wheaties, bananas, and beer.

I had a physics class in a large lecture hall at 9 a.m. on Monday, Wednesday, and Friday. Usually before class even started I'd be bent over with stomach cramps.

Now I digress: When I was in the sixth grade, my dad and his German hunting buddy each killed a bull elk in the Big Hole. One evening, Jürgen made elk tartare, which, though admittedly odd, didn't taste too bad with lots of ground-up onions and pepper and stuff; all on a Ritz cracker. I ate a ton of it. The next day in class, we sixth-graders were watching a film about something or other, and I became certain I was getting appendicitis, which my mom had made sure I should be terrified about. The pain in my guts was nearly unbearable. I was sitting in the chair doubled over as dull swords were rammed in and out of my large intestine. The lower part of my abdomen rumbled loud enough for other kids to hear, and it hurt so much that I was actually making groaning noises. I wanted to say something to the teacher, but I was too embarrassed. Instead, I decided to humiliate myself, so I farted.

I'm not trying to descend into distasteful (yet funny) comedian land here, but that was the most important fart I had ever managed. It must have lasted nearly thirty seconds, and it sounded like someone had started their lawnmower and let it idle. Da-da-da-da-da-da-da-da-da-da ... and I have never felt so mentally and physically *relieved* in my life. Even as the boys laughed and the girls cringed and said "ooooh gross!" I just kept it rattling along until all the gas caused by eating fucking raw elk meat had escaped. My complete embarrassment lost out to complete relief.

Now back in physics class nearly twenty years later, I was experiencing these same pains each Monday, Wednesday, and Friday, and although the whitetail meat hadn't been raw, I knew now it was rotten, and I knew what those pains meant, and I didn't know anyone in the class anyway, and it hurt so much. I was able to quell the sound, but each fart was so hot that it felt like my folding chair seat had its own heater, powered by a plutonium fission nuclear reactor. And they each smelled like, well, rotten whitetail deer meat; it was like being hit in the face with a shit-bat. At the start of the semester, the students sat in the auditorium in a pretty much random pattern, but within three weeks, all the students were crammed over on the left side, while I sat alone on the right. I never meant to be a dickhead, but it was almost funny releasing the pain and watching as the students would look around at each other and check the bottoms of their shoes.

At the end of the semester, the instructors always passed out fill-in-the-bubble reviews about the effectiveness of the class. There was also a section where you could write any extra comments. Being on the far side of the auditorium, the reviews were all passed to me so I could put them in the envelope and bring them to the department office. On one of the reviews was written, in the extra comment space, "You should probably check the ventilation system in this building because I think there's a dead body in it somewhere."

10—Late Season Elk

ONE OF THE OPPORTUNITIES I was afforded during those difficult college years was late-season elk hunting in both Idaho and Montana. It was an opportunity that I did not sufficiently appreciate at the time; what most concerned me by December was upping my daily beer intake above twelve cans, often seasoned with whiskey, and finishing the college semester by hook or by crook. I don't have many regrets in life, but there are a few and a solid percentage of them deal with hunting.

My dad was (and still is) obsessed with hunting to a point that makes my thoughts about it seem trivial. He is obsessed. I won't ever be able to clearly determine his motivations behind it, but I do know that he will fork over whatever time and money is needed in order to get the best opportunities possible to hunt in Idaho and Montana, on public land, and without a guide. (Being residents of either state at some point or another, nobody in my family has had the need to hire an outfitter or pay to hunt on private land, though once in awhile my dad would have to get permission to access private land—to cross it, if nothing else, onto public land. I have never purposely hunted private land as I'm not diplomatic enough). Throughout those college years, Dad always put us in for late-season cow elk hunts in the Salmon River country in Idaho, or in the Madison River country in Montana. He would do all it took to hunt as many days as possible, sparing no time or money. But he is cheap when it comes to rifles.

We were usually on Christmas break from school and back in Idaho Falls for the late elk season. The reason I did not appreciate it then was because it took time away from hangover recovery and additional partying with my back-in-the-day buddies. It has taken until now, as I write this, to fully appreciate what seemed to be just north of an annoyance back then.

The sound of the alarm raked my brain out of a stupor and with zero pity. "Fuck, I am sick of being cold and tired," I mumbled.

And oh so cold it is in December when you have to compact your body up just to go outside and start the truck. "Bar-ar-ar-ar-ar-ar-ruummm. Gunna-nunnna-nunnna ... " Does your truck sound like that when you have to rattle and groan its engine to life on a south-of-zero-degrees winter morning? And then tiptoe as fast as you can back into the house to start the coffee?

Who the hell does this? Isn't this pushing it a little—haven't we had enough hunting for the year?

Not my old man! He's still in full predator mode, whether or not anyone in the family has connected with an elk, deer, or antelope in the regular season.

This is the good stuff, this is when you're gonna see all the game, this is when you're for sure gonna get some shooting. He loves these hunts so much I wouldn't be a bit surprised to see him answer the door in a Hawaiian shirt and Bermuda shorts. Ten degrees below zero ain't shit for him, that's a hunting heat wave. Personally, I was sick of it by December; I just wanted to party. I'd hunted nearly every damn day in north Idaho, and now I just wanted to start my day holding a glass of bourbon and Coke with four ice cubes.

The old Remington Model 721 .30-06 Springfield, probably $10 or some shit when he bought it at the grocery store back in the '50s, is probably the most reliable rifle we've got in our whole family. It's like a damn Toyota Tercel or an old fuckin' Buick Roadmaster or something. I'd hate to be seen carrying it in the field, metaphorically speaking, because if it was true that other hunters actually judged you by the firearm you brought, you would rate the old aught-six as about as exciting as a sack of gravel. These kinds of cars and rifles are the exact antithesis of the Weatherbys and Corvettes of the world. This kind of equipment will speak for itself to other people. It says, "I am boring. I do everything right. I read consumer reviews, do my math homework, and save my money. I do not talk shit, or look good. I am not fun, but ... (and here's the most aggravating part), I get the job done, and done right, every time." Sadly, that's not how I usually operate. I like to operate on a champagne diet with a beer budget. I would shoot

Weatherbys and drive Corvettes all day, just give me the line of credit. I like (but I'm learning not to) spectacular endings to wild stories—or at least some moderate success from astounding failure. Those stories, when they involve hunting, should include expensive, loud, fast, fluted-barrel, composite-stocked, hair-trigger cannons, complete with a mule-kick recoil.

This morning, however, I see that Dad has a *different* rifle, one I've not seen before.

I guess because he works at a place stacked ten-deep in any given hallway with bullshitters, he is simply overwhelmed, and thus has picked a few of the bull-shittiest guys to listen to when it comes to choosing rifles in these later years. Man, they can sure market themselves and their garbage! I hadn't realized that then, so I was somewhat enamored with the single-shot "Handi-rifle" chambered in the oh-so-usual .30-06. At least the caliber was true to form, huh? I should have been skeptical when I learned "handi" was part of the name. They couldn't even spell it right. Top that off with a Simmons 44 Mag scope, and wow, what an elk-killing machine. I didn't know then that the price of this whole outfit was not a whole lot more than a tank of gas. But hey, it was a single-shot, and in my mind that made it super-accurate, and there was no easy internet then, so I bought in on it too. Leave those rusty old Remingtons and Winchesters home, forget the lightning-bolt Browning 7mm Magnum and .300 Weatherby Magnums, we've got us a single-shot .30-06 Handi-Rifle!

Even if you are a hard-partying asshole college kid, even if you hate being outdoors in December in the bitter cold, there is no way you could step from the truck in the country east of the Madison River in Montana and not be stunned by the landscape's utter magnificence. In the blackness of that last hour before dawn, the astonishing part is not terrestrial—it's cosmic. There are just so many stars. So many. The universe is *so* big. These stars almost seemed to get reflected out across the snow field where we had parked, so there were equally millions of star-snow crystals. Hard to look at that at not be thankful and forget your fatigue and hangover just for a minute.

We crunched away from the truck, through a barbed-wire fence, across a frozen creek, through icy willows, and up a steep slope. Dad, of course, had scouted this all, and he knew where the elk were likely to be; I was just a hanger-on, taking the spoils of his homework—and I just hope I can pay that forward to my boys. He pointed us upslope and east toward a darker part of dark that I knew was the beginning of the thick timber. Scattered clouds rolled through the valley and made shadows across the field of snow crystals as we crunched through. This was a uniquely beautiful sight that I had never noticed before. Dad still talks about those rolling shadows on the sparkling snow.

After a half hour of crunching through the icy snow, we stopped for a breather and began to hear them. They were barking everywhere. Cow elk make like this squeaking/barking/braying noise as their form of communication. Sometimes it's an actual bark like a dog; more often it's like a quick "Beee-yawww." Unlike bulls, who make a magnificent bugle during the early fall rut, the cows chirp and mew and talk like this all year. Maybe the bulls bark, too, I'm not sure. Either way, it fires you up because you know you're close. Now all the hangover and misery thoughts are gone. It clicks on something inside of you to where the only shaking you do is caused by nerves, no longer by the cold.

What was so utterly exciting and a total trip for me was moments later, seeing this herd of between 200 and 300 elk, making their way across the snow-crusted prairie—and on a collision course with us. You couldn't pick out any individual animals just yet, too dark, but you could just see the mass of bodies moving collectively so that it almost looked like a parade of ants across a picnic table. I'm just about shitting rocks at this point. Then we hear some crunching below and to the right of us, and I wait until my eyes can adjust to the light level in that direction, and here comes another fork of migrating animals this way! My dad and I standing on the white line of an eastbound two-lane elk interstate. "Holy shit!" I think to myself. "Get ready!"

My dad is right, these late-season hunts do get damned exciting, even if you aren't looking to score a Boone and Crockett bull. But all we can do is wait, and hope they slow up a little. The only way we can distinguish them right now is from starlight on the

116

white snow canvas. We're still nearly an hour from shooting light.

And they do slow up and meander, just as the old man said they would. They spend all night down on the flats near the river, bee-line back across the highway, and feed back up into the timber, all through the Bear Creek management area. I can hardly breathe I'm so nervous and excited. We are essentially pinned down here, not much we can do but move slowly toward the southern herd and try to find a gully or gulch to hunker down in.

By just a few minutes after dawn, we had crept to within 200 yards of the south herd, which continued its meandering flow toward the cover of the timber. This is when reality departs from that which you see on the Outdoor Channel. On TV you can edit out pot shots, misses, bad hits, and general stupidity. You can never tell exactly what's going on there. Did that fat redneck bastard really drop that bull on his first shot? Or did he more than likely miss with the first shot, trim a back leg off with the second bullet, and gut shoot it on the third? Then do a "one-shot, one-kill" to the heart and lungs after those other parts were edited out? In reality, I even think the damn bi-pods they all use on TV are a waste of money, time, and weight for the normal hunter. Who the hell ever has time to sit down and get a rest like that? Within a thousand yards of an elk, when the elk are wild? I want to hunt with you!

But here we were with the Handi-rifle, its bi-pod attached to the forestock, with me looking like a monkey trying to fuck a football as I tried to figure out how to release the legs of the damn thing, extend them, and then try to find the right extension length to fit how I wanted to make a rest to make the shot. Put the legs in the prone position, can't see over the sagebrush; put the legs up high enough and I can't sit down and see through the scope; put them at a height where I am kneeling and the elk can see my fat blaze-orange ass all day long.

Then the comedy of errors really began. Dad, impatient by both nature and training, starts grabbing at the bi-pod too, trying to help me out. I'm slapping his hands away, he's slapping at mine; we must look like two of the three stooges out here on the prairie. "Get the fu--, get awa--, ... the hell's the problem, I got this ... hang on goddammit."

Finally, I just sat in a normal position and took a normal rest to make a normal shot. Fuck that bi-pod. I think I even bent one of the legs trying to just get it out of my face. The comedy wasn't over yet. When you hunt with a partner, especially my dad, he's got to know which elk you're shooting at. There's 200+ elk over there and now I'm trying to call my shot. I haven't even decided which one I'm shooting at. I'm so excited, I'm just about ready to start herd shooting— with a single-shot rifle. But he's trying to be helpful and pragmatic, he just wants to know which one may or may not get hit.

Elk are tough animals, and often they won't even flinch after being hit hard. This can cause a hunter to illegally kill multiple animals in a situation like this because the one elk you shot first is dead already, but just doesn't know it, so it keeps running with the now-fleeing herd. You, in your excitement, think you've missed, and you forgot which one you shot at first (all of the cow elk look identical, don't they?) so you shoot at another, and maybe another. The third one drops like it was hit by a lightning bolt, the other two drop dead a couple seconds later, and now you've got a big problem!

Dad was trying to avoid that, which is good, but it was causing me to get even more rattled. "Fuck, I don't know Dad! I'm gonna shoot the brown one!"

"Goddammit, is it in the middle, the front, what? Which one?"

BANG!!! I was tired of screwing around, I knew which one I was aiming at. I think I did, anyway. At the flat crack of the rifle, the whole line of elk just stopped and started looking around.

On TV when they use single-shots, and in magazines, when you read about hunters who use single-shots, it's *all* about the sniperesque one-shot, one-kill. One single bullet, it's all you need. Not me, not this time. Here's an example of the multiplicative property of shooting errors: me, panicking x hunting partner, panicking x 200 elk, about to panic x distinct properties of calibers with respect to windage and elevation at distances greater than 100 yards x a fuckin' Handi-rifle x a toy scope x the cheapest scope bases and rings money can buy = a one-shot/one kill situation turned into the firing of a half box of .30-06 shells and one wounded cow elk with a bullet in its hoof, or as Tommy DeVito in *Goodfellas* would say, its paw.

My ears rang and the elk ran. The only thing I was happy about was that at least I didn't hit more than one elk. I'm dumb and excitable, but I can focus a little, so I knew which one I was slinging lead at the whole time. The rest of the herd quickly outdistanced my cow into the timber as she hobbled just out of sight into a small stand of timber. Geez, I hate wounding animals, but that doesn't matter right now. You've got to bury those guilt feelings. You can't be a pussy, you've got to go finish what you started.

So we followed her tracks from the first spots of blood into the timber. Thankfully, she hadn't gone out the other side and was just standing broadside to us, at about thirty yards, when we came over a rise. I pulled the hammer back (yes, the Handi-rifle has a hammer) and aimed for a spot behind the ears. POW. Nothing. She didn't move a muscle. When you break open the action on this POS rifle to shove in a fresh round, it's like trying to thread a needle with a dowel rod, but I got it done and tried again. POW. Again nothing. The elk just looked at us. "Fuck, something is the matter with this piece-of-shit rifle. You try!" I exclaimed. I handed my dad the Handi-rifle and another shell. POW. Nothing. We couldn't even see where the bullets were hitting—from just thirty yards! It was probably somewhere over by Hebgen Lake. The elk started to walk off as I handed my dad another cartridge. This time Dad walked about ten yards closer and just shot into the wheelhouse. This one finally worked, and the elk made about three big jumps and tumbled down the slope. Dead.

Yes, it was a fiasco. But if anyone tells you that every hunt and every shot is perfect, they're full of it. The thing about hunts like this is that they're the ones you remember so clearly. For the elk, it sucks, but I don't like to think about that too much, I just promise myself to try harder and do better next time. For the hunter, though, it's perfection simply if you got the opportunity to go to a place like this and see all those stars and those snow crystals and those elk and be so excited and full of adrenaline. Of course, it's good to connect and to have that meat, too, but even if you make it home and you have nothing tangible to show for it, you still have your memories, and they're yours and nobody can take them away, and they'll take you back in time and make you laugh and make you cry — and also make you make sure you use a bolt-action repeating rifle.

The country around the Salmon River is some of the most rugged and wild in North America. The vertical relief (the change in elevation from top to bottom) is 7,000 feet in some areas, even more than the Grand Canyon. That fact kept bouncing around in my tired brain as I followed my dad up the trail that ran alongside a creek, frozen over in this bitter cold, but still gurgling underneath the ice. The gurgling beckoned for me to chop a little hole in the ice and drink some of the water. We weren't even a mile from the truck yet, and it wasn't even daylight, and I was already parched. I had given up cardio workouts by this point in my life, and was only interested in power-lifting, a fact I was certain to regret in this country made for mountain-goat men.

It surely didn't help that I had sucked a dozen Milwaukee's Best beers down less than twelve hours before, and eaten a sixteen-ounce steak and a baked potato, and just a few hours ago had eaten a dozen sausages, a half-dozen pancakes, three eggs, a day-old donut, and a piece of grapefruit—a breakfast feast that my grandma had spread out on the table at 3:00 a.m. She always did this, none of us ever asked her to, she just did, and it was a "bless her heart" thing because my God, that is too much food for anyone at that time in the morning, unless you're at the buffet in Las Vegas after hours of drinking and gambling. But she worked so hard getting it ready for us that we always felt compelled to eat as much as we could and get sick to our stomachs later if truly necessary.

Now I fought all those things and played mind games with myself; and pondered yet again the sanity of my father, still wanting to hunt in the dead-ass of winter in mountain-goat land, or no-man's land. Hell, another name for the nearby Middle Fork of the Salmon River is the "River of No Return." I thought to myself, "If I happen to shoot a cow elk, and it makes it over the hill into another drainage, I won't return here to hunt."

Geez, I'm just telling you, if I could have those times back....

Anyway, it's just Dad and I trying to tromp quietly along the trail, and as the sun comes up I see just how steep these hillsides are. It's just incredible elk country, though, and I knew sure as shit we'd at least see some today. And it didn't take long.

We rounded a bend in the trail, and having hunted for so long and having trained my eyes to see stuff that's "just different" in the mountains, I looked on the opposite side of the trail, and maybe a thousand yards away there was a small band of elk feeding right out in the open above a small patch of timber. I hissed at Dad and we both sat down in the snow and pulled out the binocs. All bulls, of course—what you *invariably* see when you're packing a cow tag. Big, beautiful 6-point bulls, nine of them, just pawing at the snow to find what feed they could.

There *were* bull tags in this unit, for this time of year, but the odds of drawing one are really slim, so we always put in for cow tags, which to tell you the truth are damn near as fun to hunt. Plus, if you draw a cow, you at least have a good chance of getting out and going at all, whereas with those bad odds on the bull tags, chances are you'd be home in bed with your hangover right now or doing some other relaxing thing (given the choice at that time of year, through that time period in my life, I'd have likely put in for bull tags, hoping I *didn't* draw).

So we enjoyed the view for a moment, then stood back up, brushed the snow off our wool pants, and walked maybe fifty yards more down the trail, and rounding another bend, startled the lead cow of another herd that had been feeding on the same side of the canyon as the trail. I saw her before Dad did, so again I hissed and we quickly sat down. Even in the sitting position, I could clearly see her head and most of her neck, less than a hundred yards away. She was trying to figure out what we were, which is why we sat down. I think elk have to think about it a little when they see a human that isn't standing upright, and this can buy you a little time.

Now I make another minor digression. Evidently, the debacle of the single-shot rifle the previous year had not halted my dad's quest for a new and cheap rifle system, having been talked into another one by one of the self-proclaimed experts. This one was a Savage Model 116. It had only two things going for it: at least it was bolt-action, and at least it was a magnum cartridge: a .300 Winchester Magnum. It actually looked like a pretty cool rifle; it had a black composite stock, a fluted stainless steel barrel, and even a muzzle brake. But, oh, here we go. First, it was left-handed because my dad is a left-handed shooter, and he had talked me into using it for this hunt (yeah, why would I want to bring my new Weatherby Mark V .300 on this hunt??). Who the hell does that? What right-handed shooter uses a left-handed bolt-action rifle? I guess like Dad I can be easily talked into things. And right there on top of that rifle was mounted the same Simmons scope with the same flimsy bases and rings barely keeping it on the gun.

So I settled into a good shooting position and got ready to deliver. I am capable of making a head/neck shot on an elk at this distance, but as I was settling into position, with the cow still looking at us, Dad basically shit his pants. I promise this is the last time I will talk about farting in any other book I will ever write, but when a fart changes the outcome of my world, it deserves mention.

There are breathing techniques you employ when you're going to make a shot, and especially with a relatively difficult shot, you need to stick to them. Take a deep breath, let it out halfway, and so on. Now, as I was living in an oxygen-poor environment, the methane having forced away all my clean breathing air, I was doing all I could just to keep from passing out. I held and held my breath to avoid an uptake of airborne feces, but finally had to exhale, and I just happened to make that powerful exhale right onto the ocular lens of the Simmons toy riflescope. I don't usually keep a handkerchief in my pocket, and my first extinct was to wipe it with my leather glove, which is what I did, and that just worsened the opaque screen now in place on the scope.

If I was that cow elk, I would have enjoyed watching and listening to the two comedians below me. And watch she did, as I fumbled around and Dad hissed, "What the hell's the problem? Why aren't you shooting?"

"You shit your pants, I can't fuckin' breathe," I replied.

"Goddammit, she's gonna run, take the shot." He thought I was just being a candyass complaining about the fart.

"The problem is," and I tried to keep calm as I was hissing through gritted teeth, "when I let out the breath your fart caused me to hold, I fogged up this scope."

"Well, why didn't you tell me," he said, and he handed me the rifle he was carrying: the never-miss-always-starts-runs-great-looks-okay-bread-and-butter-Buick-Roadmaster-Remington Model 721.

But the elk was gone. The elk that, with a 75-yard shot to the face, would have quickly and easily ended a hunt that in this country could result in my hiking straight up mountains all day, all 5-feet-10-inches and 260 pounds of me, plus gear. Tom had come with us, but he'd opted to stay back at the truck to smoke cigarettes and drink Coke and nap and maybe get a shot at an easy one cruising past the truck. He may have made the correct decision.

Never pass up an easy elk, especially in the Salmon River country. This thought was pounding through my head as we worked, and I mean *worked*, our way up the sidehill following this herd's tracks. I was wishing I had just sucked up the smell, eaten shit if you will, and made the shot I'd had at that cow. It was the typical climbing scenario up a steep and snow-covered hill: take as big a step as your quadriceps muscle will allow you to, then engage your gastrocnemius muscle (your calf) on that same leg to keep you from tumbling as you slide back about half the distance that "mountain lunge" just got you.

And here I was, in another wonderful example of God's country, complaining. It was the hangover, it was my fat ass, it was too much food, it was too late in the season, it wasn't my own rifle, and it was the fact that my dad, 57 years old at the time, was kicking my 22-year-old ass at hiking. I just wanted this to be over, and I kept thinking of my lazy, yet wise, brother back at the car, sipping a Coke and smoking a Camel Light, looking over God's country from the warmth of the pickup cab.

However, there is yet another benevolent fact about elk hunting this time of year, and that is that the elk, in the never-ending battle of calories consumed versus calories burned, won't move any farther away from danger than is absolutely necessary when the temperature is sub-zero and food is in shorter supply. Elk are big into energy conservation—it's why they survive brutal winters in a place like this. We knew this, and we also knew that as soon as we crested the ridge, we'd probably bump this herd again.

Any hunter will tell you that when you're anticipating action, just after a power hike like this, it's doubly hard to catch your breath. We were so sure that the herd was nearby that I needed to stop just below the top of the hill and calm down a minute. At least I was still getting excited about this! In through the nose, out through the mouth, in through the nose, out through the mouth. Calm…. Breathe….

And sure enough, as we moved slowly in a crouched walk, over the ridgetop, into the border area where all hell could break loose at any time, one elk after another came into view. The knee-deep snow was soft and quiet, so it was relatively simple to move up to a pile of rocks that the hunting Gods put in places like this to act as natural rifle-rests. The wind was switching back and forth to our left and to our right, with that *swooshing* sound that can be almost haunting out in the middle of nowhere like this. What that wind does to me is get me more excited and more nervous. In more pragmatic terms, probably like how Dad was thinking, at least it wasn't coming from behind us and blowing our scent into the herd of about twenty animals.

Now we were in position and I was trying to pick out a cow away from the rest of the herd to shoot at. "Which one are you aiming at?" Dad asked. Oh God, here we go again.

But now I had a brand-new and never-before-encountered problem. When I looked through the scope I could either clearly see the magnified elk and the crosshairs weren't visible, or I could clearly see the crosshairs, but the elk were blurry — too blurry to pick out where on the body to shoot, at 200+ yards. Trying to articulate this to my dad in hissed whispers was like trying to wipe your butt with boxing gloves on — it just wasn't going to happen. So I picked the clear-crosshairs-blurry-elk option and starting shooting.

BANG! Miss. The bullet kicked snow and dirt up just below the cow I was shooting at, so at least Dad now knew that much. I was able to squeeze off two more rounds as the herd started to accelerate to the right and over into the next canyon. The cow I'd been shooting at was right in the middle of the herd, but above the others on the slope, which is a good thing, because I usually try to aim for the lead cow, and that one was already over the hill.

Just as I was jacking in my fourth round POW! Dad made a beautiful shot with the 721 on the galloping cow — perfect placement, right in the firebox. You could hear the distinct thud of a solid hit and the cow immediately starting running sideways, faster, looser, and head held higher ... and then she was rolling. "Better shoot again!" I exclaimed, "Before she gets into the next canyon!" I knew goddamn well who'd be packing this animal out.

No need for follow-up shots with bullet placement like that, though. It was over quickly and the cow was sliding down through the bowl, leaving a blood and dirt trail behind. She finally stuck up on a clump of brush, and now elk-on-the-hoof was one step closer to elk in the freezer.

As always though, there is work, varying in degree depending on quite a few different factors. If you asked me today how hard I thought the packout was going to be, I'd borrow from baseball terminology and say, "A can of corn," i.e. an easy (pack) out. That time in my life, that day, was different. I'd put it at moderate to extremely difficult, and that's because it was hard enough then to just pack my own ass, let alone the weight of elk meat and gear.

After field-dressing and cutting the elk in half, we returned the mile or so to the truck to pick up a pack-board—an aluminum frame, about the height of the distance from your butt to a few inches above your head, and about shoulder width, with backpack straps, along with an orange plastic snow sled. And, hopefully, we'd get Tom to help us.

Packing out an elk in the Salmon River Country

At age twenty-two, if I were a truck, I'd say I had a Ford F-250 frame, but at best a 302 c.i. F-150 engine. Or maybe a V-6 Ford Ranger engine. To clarify, in terms of strength, I could move a lot of weight, but quite slowly and at very high RPMs, requiring a lot of fuel and oil. I was bench-pressing well over 400 lbs. then, and squatting over 500 lbs., but to time me in a mile's run would have required a calendar. Very quickly in the packout, I realized it would be best if I just put the front half of the elk on my back in the pack-board and dragged the other half on the sled — and I still got back to the truck before my dad and brother did. It was quite a feat, but it came with a cost. In the long term, I don't think my back has ever returned to normal, and in the short term, I was so thirsty that in the few hours after we were all packed up and headed back to our motel room in North Fork, I drank two gallons of orange juice.

Tom, Dad, and I back at the truck
after packing out a Salmon Country elk.

You know, maybe it was because there was only that single two-bed room available, or maybe because my dad thought Tom and I were still little kids, or maybe, well, I don't know, I guess I was too tired after that packout to sleep on the floor, but whatever — I agreed to sleep in the same bed with my brother. We had spent last night at Grandma and Grandpa's in

Anaconda, but had decided to do the motel thing because it was so late in the day when we had finished with the elk. And as unintended payback for all the times he had violently sunk an elbow into my chest when we had to sleep in the same bed as kids, or all the times he had snuck into my room at Grandma's house and turned up the electric blanket to "nuclear high" during the middle of the night, I peed the bed in the middle of this night, and I peed all over him—two gallons of processed orange juice. I remember the dream I was having as I aimed into the toilet that existed only in my unconscious mind; and I peed and peed and peed, the toilet was nearly overflowing, I was beginning to worry, when....

"Goddammit, you pissed all over me! Wake up! You pissed the fuckin' bed dude, and you pissed all over me!"

11—The Valley Floor

On one of my very first Idaho elk hunts as a 12-year-old legal rifle-toting youngster, Dad and I sat above a small patch of timber and watched a clearing and waited for a bull to come through. We were in the Weber Creek drainage of the Medicine Lodge area. Idaho used to do this rifle elk season over a period of five days, and any bull was legal. Hunters used to call it the 5-Day War, and this was not far from accurate because as soon as it was light enough to shoot, there'd be so much shooting coming from all over the place that it sounded like there were about ten giant popcorn poppers going off—that was *everyone else* getting in on the shooting. In the years in which I participated in the 5-Day War, I never once got to be one of the people banging away as the sun rose.

On that first day, though, after I'd glassed and looked over every sagebrush and every rock fifty times, making sure it wasn't an elk, I began to put the binocs out to farther distances. Heart Mountain was there even back then, twenty-six years ago, as it had been for probably at least 15 million years—quiet and cold and windy, with wisps of snow always blowing off its peak, even on the blue-sky warm October days. I looked clear over toward the mountain, and then I scanned back in closer, looking at the animal moving near our truck far down below us in the valley. "Must be a rancher's cow," I thought at first, but then I realized I was looking at a 6-point bull elk as it hobbled past our parked truck, no more than fifty yards away from the driver's side door. It was definitely an "I can't believe my eyes" moment. It had obviously taken a bullet to one of its back legs, but it was still moving, and now so were Dad and I. We came off that mountain like a couple of rolling boulders. It may have been a wounded elk, but it wasn't in any hunter's possession yet, so we still had as much right to it as the next guy.

We searched and searched through all the sagebrush draws and little rocky gulches for the rest of the day, looking for the bull himself, or at least a trail of blood. We found nothing, but damn, it was exciting. That was 1987. Guns and hunting were my favorite things in the world, occupying at least 75 percent of my thoughts on any given day.

By the fall of 1998, though, I was just about to be done with the sport forever. In the spring of 1997, I had experienced first-hand, and in real-time, the pale horror of clinical mental illness. There is being nervous about stuff, and there is feeling anxious about stuff, there are anxiety issues, and then there's post-traumatic stress disorder (PTSD). Blame it on a buildup of the issues that a lot of people will go through in life, blame it on genetics, blame it on overuse of alcohol and the blur of daily self-medication, but whatever you do, don't blame the person. This is bad stuff.

I woke up one night, about a week after my constant companion and best friend died (it was a dog, of course, I don't get along with humans nearly as well), and I knew something wasn't right. It's even hard to write about and describe here because of the fear it could return, but if I could explain that night, it was as if something had invaded my brain and was now the one calling the shots. There was some kind of bad motherfucker at the wheel; it did not have my best mental interests in mind, and it was ruthless.

I lay there in the darkness and felt like I was kind of in this dark bubble and I couldn't catch my breath. There were the standard anxiety attack symptoms (the feeling like you're dying, etc.), but these things that I know about now, in my late thirties, were then unfamiliar and terrifying to me in my early twenties. I didn't know how to ask for help, and I didn't even know if I should. I had always felt in total control of myself, and now how was I supposed to go tell someone that I had lost that control? You don't get heart attacks at age 21 when you're in relatively decent shape, yet that's what I felt like I was having at least three times a day. You don't die from "nothing," so what the fuck was killing me? Who do you even ask for help? Parents will just blame it on your laziness or your drinking problem, or the fact that you don't go to church as often as you should.

What it boiled down to was reclaiming control of myself, and in the end, since this is a hunting story, the manifestation of this mental illness regarding hunting was that I no longer felt like I should hold a gun in my hands. I felt that having the power to end it all was the most powerful control switch there was, and a .30-06 Springfield and a .357 Magnum were no longer tools of a fun activity, but rather, they represented the eject button from a life that had lost the rudder and throttle control linkages.

On top of that, for a short time there, I became like one of the Hindu practitioners of *ahimsa*, who believe that to hurt another living being is to hurt oneself. I did not wish any more pain on myself and certainly not on any living thing, especially furry creatures with brown eyes.

I did have friends in Moscow who still wanted to hunt, though, so I still went, but I'd be drinking beer by 5:00 in the morning, and we tried to do all our hunting from the truck. I mean, how far are you going to hike after you've drunk a dozen beers? One morning I went to pick up one of my buddies to take him whitetail hunting and he answered the door in pajamas.

"What the hell are you doing, Brian?" I asked.

"Come here for a second, I wanna show you something," he said.

He took me into his computer room and introduced me to one of the earliest iterations of Cabela's "Big Game Hunter" video game.

"Look here," he said, "you can hunt anywhere in the world you want and you never even have to leave home!"

Shit, he did have a point. Why get all cold and miserable just so you can maybe kill some harmless creature that never did anything to you? Why get up early in the morning so you can catch the herd before they hit the thick timber for the day, when you can "hunt" at 10 o'clock at night, three-sheets-to-the-wind drunk on a case (or so) of beer?

And I worked my way further down to the valley floor.

How ironic was it then, that as a graduation present in 1999 my dad bought the entire Montana hunting license package for me? And how ironic was it that, as a favor to try to help me pull my shit together, one of my best friends, Cory, talked me into buying an Idaho license that year as well? He got my license number from me, put us in on a "team hunt" for a special-draw lottery tag in one of the premier mule deer units in the entire world? When you put in for those team hunts, or "buddy hunts," and one of you draws a tag, the other person automatically gets a tag as well. He drew.

So as I descended into a valley floor of way too much partying and way too little thought about one of my favorite activities in the world, I was "saddled" with a couple of the finest public-land unguided hunting opportunities I had ever known.

I'm just telling you, if I could have those times back....

As the 1999 dream season approached, I worked my level best to prepare for it. I talked to my buddies who amped me up. I cut back drinking to only six and a half days a week, I bought a Honda Fourtrax, and I practiced shooting my Weatherby rifle at least two times a week. I even went out to the desert west of town and shot a rabbit, just so I could try to renew some blood thirst. I bought the best hunting clothes I could afford, and every night pored over maps of Montana and Unit 69 in Idaho. I would go here and here and here and here ... I will hold out for a 350-class bull in Montana, and a 200+ B&C mule deer in Idaho. The Beartooth Mountains, the Absarokas, the Clark Fork, Bull's Fork, Brockman Creek, Rock Creek, and the Gravelly Range!

Then my girlfriend left me for another guy, I realized I was flat-ass broke, I was a drunk, and now here I was in the fuckin' Big Hole with my non-drinking all-business dad and his German hunting buddy. Exactly where the fuck did I go wrong here? This was going to make me hunt in the Crazy Mountains! You can't kill an elk in the Big Hole! You especially won't be looking over multiple herds of elk and saying shit like they do on the Outdoor Channel, "The G-6's on that bull are lacking. That other bull there, he has good mass, but doesn't have much spread, 290 at best."

No, if you are exceedingly skillful and damn lucky, you might get a snap shot at a raghorn as he slams through the lodgepole at thirty miles an hour! There's plenty of elk there, but this isn't Hollywood Hunting. "Oh well," I thought, "fuck it, there's plenty of beer, and Jürgen will drink with me."

And I drank beer all night, just sitting in my Chevy truck, listening to the only tape I had brought with me, Phil Collins' *Serious Hits... Live!* I wonder whatever happened to my Dire Straits tape?

When my dad started stirring in the predawn hours, making and drinking coffee and eating a doughnut, while I poured a can of V8 into a red Solo cup already half full of Bud Light, I did have a fleeting thought and memory about how exciting and fun hunting had been back in 1987 and '86 and '85, and even more fun before that.

Being sober and nearby someone who's drunk is unsettling at best, infuriating at worst; so it should have come as no surprise that my dad was going to say something about this, and soon.

"What the fuck is the matter with you?" he asked. "You used to like this stuff. You used to take this seriously. Now you've pretty much blown the opening day for all of us, getting shitfaced all night and acting like an asshole."

The problem with talking to a drunk person like that is that there's no way that kind of language is not going to be perceived as a challenge. What did he expect me to say? "You know Dad, you're right! I'm going to stop right now. I am sorry if I have offended you. Let us go have a nice day in the woods."

I think he knew better than that, my dad likes a good fight, and so do I, because for some reason in my family the protocol is to have a helluva fight and then make up after a little while. So what I said in response was, "Fuck you, old man. Do you think I'm your bitch? Do you think I have to do every goddamn thing you tell me to do? I know this country better than you. I'm a better hunter than you. I could outhike, outlift, outfight, and outshoot you any fucking day of the week — drunk, sober, or hungover."

I yelled those slurred words to him about two inches from his face, and they echoed through the timber of the Pioneer Mountains — my dad, his buddy Jürgen, and I the only humans for miles and miles and miles around. Opening day of the 1999 Montana elk hunting season and I was holding a shovel in my hands waiting to brawl with my dad. A pop of sparks shot out from the fire, which was still crackling as it cast a shadow in the pitch darkness of 4 in the morning on the tents and the trucks and this unreal and totally absurd scene.

Fortunately hunting is our common ground, so after a five-minute stare-down that probably made Jürgen wonder just what in the hell he had gotten himself into ("crazy goddamn Americans" he said later), we thumped the campfire and shouldered our packs and rifles. At that point, my dad just did not understand my issues, nor did I understand his. It's that age-old father-son dilemma.

"Point A" is the name of the GPS-marked secret spot you've got to be at on opening morning at the head of Squaw Creek. It's your Obi-Wan (only hope) for an easy elk in this country because when dawn breaks, the shooting starts below you in the foothills, marked in my GPS as "Shooting Gallery." The elk will follow this certain escape route *one time* back into the deepest, darkest timber in Montana. They won't come this way again, on purpose, at least as far as our family knows after fifty years of scouting and hunting here. Point A is located in a saddle in some scattered timber where you can see about fifty yards — and that's long-range shooting in the Big Hole!

We hiked in silence to Point A; silence because that's what you do when you hunt, and silence because each of us was wondering what in the hell had just happened, and silence because I no longer wanted to be here. I no longer gave a damn about hunting, and when the shooting started just after the timber turned gray and the stars started to blink out, I never felt even a skosh of excitement or anticipation. I was so physically and mentally sick that when the cracking started in the timber (a spine-tingling harbinger of the shit about to hit the fan), as the elk made their way through the escape route, I didn't even click my rifle's safety in the FIRE position.

And I generally have bad luck, so all that came by me were five cows and calves. Just out of my sight there had been more timber cracking and not too long after that a KAPOW!! from another hunter's rifle, someone who had also somehow discovered this escape route. The six-point had gone to him and not me. I didn't care. I just missed my now-ex-girlfriend and needed a beer.

In all, we spent a week in the Big Hole, and just when you think that maybe I had sobered up for the rest of the week, think again; airline liquor bottles fit nicely into hunting backpacks, and NyQuil will buzz you up too. I never did see another elk that trip, or deer, or anything that I specifically recall. I pretty much became blind to all that was occurring in the present, but with crystal vision to the past. Future? Not much. When a hobby you've always loved like I had always loved hunting becomes just another excuse to drink at best, something you dread at worst, it's time to find something new to do. How ironic then, that on Monday following this hell week, it was the opening day of one of the finest special-draw hunts in the country?

Every Idaho hunter I personally know puts in for the lottery to draw this deer hunt, every year. Idaho Fish and Game will usually draw somewhere around ten tags, with like 800 applications. How's that for odds: 1 in 80. You don't have much more than a 1 percent chance of drawing, and here I was holding one of those tags! Here I was holding one of those tags in one hand and a beer in the other. I didn't even care anymore, but because Cory had done this for me, I intended to put on at least some kind of act.

It's early November now as I meet my buddy in the K-Mart parking lot around 4:00 in the morning. Under the parking lot mercury lights we move all kinds of hunting gear from his truck to mine. There's packs and rifles and ropes and binocs and lunches, coats and gloves and hats and knives. This seems like it'd be a sport for the minimalist, and indeed many old-timers did it that way, with a rifle and knife and a rope. But we love our gear these days. We love this kind of gear so much that, hell, camouflage is a mainstream fashion statement now!

There are only patches of snow here and there, which is bad for two reasons: one, the herd of deer that this hunt is intended to thin (by ten bucks) is a migratory herd, and they won't move into this country from the relative safety of the mountains and forests south of Palisades Reservoir unless driven by weather, and two, the Tex Creek WMA/Skyline Ridge/Kep's Crossing road is a sonofabitch when it's muddy. I've got bald tires on the Chevy, chains that don't quite fit, and cellphones were in 1999 not yet common. Oh well, there's my buddy and there's beer.

I had heard that this hunt was the closest thing to what you see on hunting TV shows these days. There were supposedly so many deer and so many nice bucks that you'd be forced to choose and "field-judge" them to determine how close a buck was to making the record book. Instead, what we got as daylight came closer and closer was gusting winds and pelting snow that drove sideways across the windshield and the hood of the truck. It came in sheets, and I was having to really pay attention to what I was doing as a driver because the Skyline Ridge Road was already turning into a slippery mess. Where there weren't big drifts left over from previous storms, there were stretches of road so slick and muddy that I could turn my steering wheel hard to the left and the truck just continued straight ahead. I was making rooster-tails of gumbo with all four tires, even here on the main road. I began to get so nervous about driving that my stomach was getting a little sick. In some places there were big drop-offs, like cliff drop-offs, and if you slid off one of those you were dead. In other places if you slid off, you were just basically screwed for the day, until maybe it cooled off and the mud froze solid again.

By 8:00 in the morning, I was ready for a beer. My nerves were shot. Fuck this. By the end of opening day I knew that the only way I was gonna get any shooting on this hunt was if a buck, any buck (I had now made the decision to shoot the first deer I saw that had bone on the brain) jumped out from somewhere and just stood there.

I returned back home to Idaho Falls that night with nerves so rattled that even all the beer I had drunk hadn't fazed me.

What had happened to me? I did used to love this stuff! Four years ago I would have slammed and dug my truck through that mud and snow like a kid playing with a big toy. I would have hiked and slogged up and down these mountains and through these beautiful aspen and timber patches all damn day for a deer. I would have eaten this shit up! Now I was acting like a wounded and scared little bitch.

Mercifully the last day of the season arrived. Because this hunt is such a big deal, I was continually pestered by people to return, like every other day. My friends just wanted to be along on this hunt, it was considered such a gem. Another irony of the whole mess was that I now had a bachelor's degree in wildlife management, yet I hated hunting—my world was all kinds of bass-ackwards. On top of everything else, and this *is* funny, I had to sell my Leupold rifle scope to the pawn shop in order to pay for gas and beer for this last hunt. I did that the day before this last day of the season, and I was too prideful to ask my dad to borrow one of his rifles (and you *never* borrow a rifle from someone who isn't family or that you can't pay to replace), so when I pulled my Weatherby Mark V Weathermark .300 Winchester Magnum out of its $150 case, it had only the scope rings on it. I figured I could use those as decent open sights for a short range shot that I didn't care if I got anyway. My two buddies saw that and ended up bent over from laughter for about ten minutes. When I think about it now, it really is pretty comical.

Considering my mental circumstances at that point, I guess I did try pretty hard to find a buck on that last day. The weather hadn't been bad enough to push the big migratory herd from Unit 67 into this unit, but there is a resident herd that tools around the lower foothills south of Ririe Reservoir. In all, we saw ten deer that last day, all women and children. So with a crack of a beer from the cooler, we headed toward town in the late afternoon. The can of beer had dried mud all over it, so a couple of swigs came with dirt.

I was thinking about that dirt, and wondering what it did to my teeth. Does it help clean them? Or does it wear them down? This is what I was pondering when we rounded what is literally the last bend in the road before you're out of hunting country. My buddy Aaron was driving and he had to skid my Chevy to a stop when the herd busted out of the willows on the left side of the road, bounded across it, and headed out into a stubble field. The last deer was a big forkedhorn buck, and I mean a big one. I'll bet the spread on that bastard's rack was twenty-five inches. It was the biggest 2-point I had ever seen. This unit has great genetics.

I had one last bit of motivation in me, or maybe it was just instinctual prey drive.

"Get out, get out! Let me get my rifle!"

We all bailed out and I fished the Weatherby out from behind the seat. Usually I would have had it uncased and in my lap, but I had really been hoping we were done hunting.

There were probably about a dozen deer in this herd, including the 2-point buck. By the time we had stopped and bailed out, they had made it out to about 200 yards when Aaron whistled. Mule deer, bless their doltish hearts, will stop and look back at strange sounds like that (I once stopped a fleeing doe by meowing like a cat). They were all milling around wondering whether they should be scared or not. ("Did you hear a noise? I heard a noise.") I was kneeling in the soft dirt and readying for a shot when

146

the big forkedhorn moved off to the left by himself for a second.

I'm a decent shot, but sighting through scope rings? I think I was really hoping I'd miss when I pulled the trigger. Nope. Ker-Slap! You could hear the thud as the 180-grain Nosler slammed home. It was poor sportsmanship, though, to make a shot with a rifle with no real sights, and sadly, the deer paid for my bush-league action. It humped up and did the telltale tippy-toe run that you usually see with a gut-shot animal. It was headed at an angle away from us, back toward the road.

It was that moment that I knew I was done with this business. I couldn't shoot anymore to finish the job, so I did another spineless act and handed Bryce my rifle. "Finish him off, dude. I just can't do it," I said.

He emptied the rest of the magazine in the general direction of the hapless buck, but it still disappeared back into the willows whence it had come. The day quickly went from afternoon into the gloaming, then full darkness.

We followed the buck for probably four hours, using a flashlight to find increasingly rare spots of blood. I kept hoping and hoping to find it dead, because there was no way I'd be able to see to do a kill shot if it ran. We all finally had had enough and returned to the truck, hoping that maybe it was just a grazing wound and the deer would live to be shot at the following year.

The next day was December 1, and it snowed and snowed and snowed. I sat at home and was glad I was not out there hunting in that shit, but I felt like a total dickhead for wounding that deer. "Enough," I thought to myself. "That is *enough*. I am going to try a new hobby." And for the next six years my rifles got dusty and my knives got dull. I used my Cabela's duffel bag to store books, and I threw away my hunting clothes after it was clear I was literally outgrowing them. I lost my backpack and my Sorel boots. My binocs disappeared as well. It was over.

12—A Shot at Redemption

THERE IS ONE NASTY SECRET that I kept in my
hunting closet through those six years. I had never
killed a bull elk. To all my friends, this may (or may
not) come as a surprise because to hear me tell it
around the lunch table in junior high and high school,
I had killed a 6-point every year I'd ever been hunting.
Secrets like this are like little Dostoyevsky-like mental
tumors (on a serious note), more like a girl you never
had the balls to ask out on a date (on a lighter note).
These thoughts grow and grow until you either admit
them to yourself and to other people, or you somehow
make it right. Yes, I had given up the actual pursuit of
big game for the time being, but the nagging thought
of never bagging that 6-point, or making it right with
my old man and the mountains and the deer and the
elk and the antelope must have eaten at my
subconscious. Hunting seasons came and went, and
even though I lived in Utah then, there were still real
hunters to talk with, and I was still legally an Idaho
resident, and Idaho and Montana were still there.

But now it's 2005 and I'm hiking up the same
extremely steep and timbered sidehill in Idaho's Unit
50 that I came down in 1992 nearly as dead as the deer
I was trying to drag out. I really and truly feel good
about myself in this country. I guess I could say I feel

great today, and I feel like I have come full circle. The rifle I'm carrying is the same Winchester Model 70 I've been carrying since I was twelve years old; the scopeless .300 Mag is in a dusty old case underneath my bed. These trees are the same trees that were here when I used to hunt this country thirteen years ago. The dirt's the same, the rocks are the same, and the mountains are the same. These physical features of the land aren't just sitting there, they're anchoring me; they're sheltering me against physical *and* mental storms. They're my friends who are more than forgiving, but who don't put up with any shit either.

When I was going through the mental hell of PTSD in 1997, my brother (the same brother I had pissed all over) tried to help me by saying to me, "Just look around you—nothing has changed. I'm still the same. Your truck is still the same, your clothes are the same, it's Tuesday today, and it'll be Tuesday again in a week. The sun came up today and it'll go down tonight. Then it'll come up tomorrow again. Everything's okay, the world's still turning. All of this is *just in your mind*." I wanted to kick his ass right then. I wanted to kick everyone's ass. *Nothing* was the same, it was all different now and it always would be. I thought.

I heard his words then, but I was listening to them for the first time on this fine fall day. Yes, those quaking aspen alongside the road down there are the same aspens I hiked through a long time ago, and every year their leaves will turn into this splendid painting on Earth's canvas. Every year. These mountains and forests will wait for you, they aren't flighty and flaky — they're as solid as, well, rock.

And just as surely as those aspens go through their annual cycle, the deer will follow their diurnal cycle and start appearing quietly out of the timber patches on the other side of this ridge. By now our family has taken at least ten decent bucks out of the canyon I'll be glassing just as soon as I can get my fat ass up and over this sidehill. That's what brought me back to this country, because although I haven't accomplished any kind of hunting redemption yet, at least I'm here.

Nothing with mental illness disappears instantly and forever, but sometimes there are those days. Days like this. Days where you realize you've been clenching your teeth since you woke up, and so you relax your jaw. The world here is so big and can be so beautiful, if you let it, that it will lift the weight directly off your shoulders, and even though you'll return to your normal life on Monday, you can store the feelings of days like this like money in the bank, and use them to buy more pleasant thoughts when the normal bullshit of life thinks it can get to you.

I'm also here because I've been married now for more than two years, and my wife and stepson have looked through the old hunting albums and seen the pictures from "back in the day." They asked me why I don't do that anymore. They said it looked like I was happy. And the kicker: my wife said it's *sexy* when a man can prove to his family that no matter what happened in the world, he could still provide food for the table with his rifle. *Sexy*?

I've never thought of hunting as sexy. I've thought of *rifles* as sexy (you ain't a real rifleman if you haven't held a Weatherby Mark V rifle and wondered if you were gonna pop a hard-on right there in the gun store), but I've never thought of fur and guts and blood and cold weather and a lot of hard work as sexy — character-building, sure, but not sexy. But my wife said it was sexy, so I bought a damn deer tag. Now even though I am just drinking in all this scenery and this fresh air and this freedom and this silence, I do realize that I oughta try to get a deer.

I crest the same old ridge and move quietly down to the same old patch of rocks that overlooks two large tracts of timber. There is a long gulch that separates these two tracts, and it contains plenty of nice tall grass, or whatever the hell the deer like to eat there (evidently I didn't pay attention to that subject in class up at U of I). The sky is a perfect azure color, with some jet contrails slicing through it way high up there. The sun is starting to relax and head down, but I'd still call this pure afternoon, and it warms my back as I glass the same old topography looking for brand new deer.

I'm so surprisingly comfortable that I start to doze off a little, opening my eyes occasionally to scan the edges of the timber below me. That's where you usually see deer first; they like to hang out close to the safety zone of the thick timber before they fully expose themselves. This is why it surprises me that a little buck has made its way out from the main timber into a little copse of two or three stunted pines and aspens without my seeing it.

It's born into predators, into hunters, to change thoughts and actions instantly in these situations. It would be so cool to understand the chemical change that occurs in your brain when you see prey. One minute I was nodding off in the pleasant late afternoon, dozing in October sunlight. The next I was fully and completely focused on this deer. I had almost a full tunnel vision and laser concentration. It's not just me; it's every hunter in this situation. It would look like a tiger crouched in the bushes.

I had no need to put the binoculars on this deer, as it wasn't too much over a hundred yards away from my position. It was a little buck with an odd rack: a spike on one side, and three little points on the other. It was browsing away peacefully as I found it in my crosshairs. Evidently it's *sexy* to bring home the bacon, so I made the shot. I did not intend to come home to my wife empty-handed from the first hunting trip I'd been on since we were married. We hadn't been together long enough for me to explain, or demonstrate, to her that every hunting trip is not a killing trip—and that more often than not you don't get anything. Nope, I intended to show her that I was a predator machine. So I didn't feel sad at all when the deer simply disappeared from view at the crack of the rifle. I am certain that it did not feel a thing.

When I hiked down to it, I learned that I was still a decent shot, at least. I had aimed for a spot right between the buck's eyes, and that's where I had placed the bullet. It took me ten minutes of rooting around in the brush to find the three-point side of its antler, which had been separated from the rest of the skull by the 180-grain Silvertip. Before I started field dressing the deer, I sat down next to it in the brush, with my feet pointed straight down the hill and my hand holding my Buck knife resting on the buck's gray coat. I needed to do some introspection for a second, on a deep level, to consider and ponder why and how I am able and supposed to kill deer, and on a more pragmatic level, to remember how to gut one of these things out.

In my more-or-less educated opinion, it's morally acceptable and biologically sound to remove a scientifically determined number of deer from a herd. Keeping animal population numbers at a pre-determined level ensures health of the entire herd. The sales of hunting licenses and tags is really the only revenue that state fish and game departments have to work with to manage these herds; typically, Western states do not contribute from the general fund to wildlife and habitat management—so in a very true sense, the thing that ensures these deer populations remain viable is the fact that they are fun to hunt and good to eat.

I felt proud of myself, too. I've already made it clear that I had actually intended to never hunt again, but I'm glad I let that go. This is a good thing. Done correctly, hunting is a clean and pure activity, and even though it often ends in the death of one thing, ultimately this death of one thing provides life for another. I didn't shoot this deer in the guts through scope rings off the side of the road; I hiked my fat ass off to get here, waited patiently, and made a clean shot. The difference between what I did in 1999 and what I did here was just vast. That was something to be ashamed of; this was something to be proud of.

Field-dressing a deer is just a different way of saying you gotta remove its guts. To do this, I wrestled the buck onto his back with his belly and chest pointing straight up. Then I took a length of rope and tied it to one of the stunted little aspens he was lying next to. The other end I ran through a slit I had cut through the gap between his Achilles tendon and his hock on the right hind leg. This would help stretch the deer's body and prop it (I can't refer to the deer as him anymore) open. Then I took a couple seconds to remember that my dad always told me this is one of the most dangerous parts of hunting: steep sidehill, uneven footing, floppy dead deer, and *very sharp knife*! "Watch what the hell you're doing!"

Next you deal with its penis, and you remove it most of the way by kind of skinning down from above it, and continuing this until it's skinned all the way back to near its right hind quarter; out of the way, but still attached, as per Fish and Game Department rules that you must keep evidence of gender on the body in case the body isn't attached to the head after you're done field dressing it and preparing it for the pack or drag out.

Then you work from where you started that skin job, and continue to skin up, out, and down. Unless you're gonna use its hide (which in taxidermy terms is called a cape) on a shoulder mount, you can go ahead and skin clear up to the throat. After this, you start back near the bottom and make a shallow slit with your knife. Here's where you gotta be careful because if you push that knife in too far, you're gonna hear a pfffffssssss, which is all the gas escaping from its now punctured gut. Not only can that produce a knock-you-down stench, it also can result in bad bacteria all over good meat (as we know from one of my previous experiences).

Next, you stick your index and middle finger into that slit, and like a surgeon with a scalpel, you make a shallow cut all the way up the hide of that abdominal cavity until you hit the base of the ribs (the breastbone). With your knife in one hand, you reach both hands up into the cavity and cut through the diaphragm (that thin sheet of tough muscle that separates the chest cavity from the abdominal cavity) all the way around. You must be super careful to not cut yourself because with your hands and forearms in the deer, you can't see your knife. Go slow, and kind of pull and slice until the whole gut pile just rolls out. It helps if you're on a sidehill like this, and its head is aimed uphill, because then gravity will help you remove that gut pile. Kick the pile away from your work area so you don't keep stepping in it.

You've now given the crows and ravens and coyotes, and maybe wolves and bears, a damn nice treat. If this was grizzly bear country, you might want to look up and around once in a while, so you don't go from predator to prey. I've heard stories about elk hunters around the boundaries of Yellowstone National Park who've had run-ins with grizzlies at gut piles because the bears will key in to the sound of gunshots and move toward them. It's like a dinner bell to those big bastards.

Anyway, now that its guts are removed, you need to reach up as far into its throat as you can and sever the windpipe (trachea). This way you can remove the heart and lungs all in one nice package and either keep them for yourself (or a friend) or throw them out with the rest of the gut pile for the scavengers.

Because I was out of practice, all of the above took me probably an hour. I could have gotten it done faster, but I also could have cut myself. I sat back down almost where I'd sat before I started, and I felt pretty good about myself. Not only did I hike in here, make a good shot, and do a good job of prepping deer on the hoof for deer in the freezer and on the grill, I also didn't think for one second about trying to retrace and relive the glory of 1992 when I damn near died trying to get a buck down the timbered slope on the other side there. I would come back tomorrow with a pack-board to get this deer off the mountain.

I propped the chest cavity open with a solid stick so it would keep cool, and took off back toward the truck. I was two-thirds of the way done with a successful hunt, and maybe a seed had been planted.

13—Easy Cow

NOW THAT I'D MADE A SEXY FIRST STEP back into hunting, I decided the next year to try my luck at the Idaho special-draw hunt lottery. It works like this: there are certain places and times of year when your chances of bagging an animal are higher than in others. The "others" are the general areas and general seasons where and when any Idaho-licensed hunter can pursue big game with a tag purchased over-the-counter. The special draw tags require additional application fees and good luck, but if you draw one, your chances of successfully harvesting an animal are something like 1 in 5, as opposed to 1 in 20 in a general season. The caveat is that to gain membership in this 1-in-5 club, you've got to be successful at winning the 1-in-8000-chance lottery. As I write this, I have put my name into the lottery for deer, elk, and antelope for a total of twenty-four years, that's seventy-two applications I've filled out, and I think I've drawn maybe six times. It's frustrating.

So when my envelope from the Idaho Fish and Game Department arrived, with something like "Congratulations, your license has been drawn for special hunt # ------, species: antlerless elk" on the sheet of paper inside, I was more than mildly pleased. I can't say I was overjoyed; I just wasn't quite in that frame of mind yet, but the feelings did stir. Also, these envelopes arrive in July, in high summer when my thoughts usually revolved around cold beer and shade and baseball, and green leaves and lawns and forest fires rather than frigid mornings colored with brown sagebrush, brown rifle stocks, and brown animals.

Opening day came and went, but I didn't. To say the old man was pissed off is an understatement. I had promised to take him with me, and now I backed out. To him, it must have seemed like both his boys had turned into pussies. The year before had been my brother's more or less official last year to hunt. Tom had drawn a damn good permit for a bull in the Island Park area, and in the frosty morning when the four-wheelers were idling as we strapped on our gear to help him hunt it, my dad asked him where his rifle was. Tom then reached into his coat pocket and produced a .22 Derringer, the kind poker players in the Old West packed, and when my dad asked, "What the hell is that? Where's your .30-06?" Tom just replied, "It's all shot placement, old man." Evidently Tom had never had any plans to hunt this bull, and this was his final dramatic "fuck this" overstatement.

So the first weekend of my hunt came and went, and I did not; and same for the next weekend. Dad kept calling and asking, "So when we gonna go get that elk?"

To which I would respond, "I think next weekend I should have time."

And the next weekend came and went, and I didn't, leaving one last weekend. The snow had fallen by now. My dad, the most aggressive hunter I have ever known, had scouted the country already up and down, inside and out. He didn't even have the tag, yet he had gone into the unit several times just to look for elk for me. It was now late November, and every morning there was a carpet of frost on the lawn and my truck was starting to groan in the cold mornings when I started it. On my way to Pocatello to school each day, I would regularly see legs of dead elk sticking out of pickup beds traveling down I-15. I sighed and thought "Well, I guess I better go get that elk." What had happened to sexy?

The morning comes early again. And again my truck groans to life, but today I'm just heading over to my dad's house and there I'll move all my gear over to his blue Dodge pickup, which I'm sure is already idling in his driveway. Gail, my dad's wife, is going with us today, which is good because she tends to mellow out the old man.

I need a mellow old man now because I'm just testing out the waters of hunting again. I'm not driven to hike and glass and work and stalk all day just so I might get a shot. Dad is retired now, so maybe he's mellowed out some about hunting. As I transfer my gear into the back seat of the Dodge, I'm kind of having both new and old feelings. Seeing my dad in those damn wool pants he wears that are so short it looks like he's waiting for a flood brings me back to the '80s, as do his red suspenders and what I'm pretty certain is the same light green Stanley thermos that used to sit down by the gearshift lever on the Bronco on our way to Montana. I'm also pretty certain these are the same stars that dotted the pre-dawn sky when Dad and Gramps and Stan and Tom and I packed into the Bronco back then. I wonder which of the five of us used to notice those stars. I know I didn't, and I doubt Tom did, but I doubt I'll ever know if the other three older guys did or not. I'm not naïve enough to think that Stan and Gramps are up there in those stars "looking down on us and smiling." The only place I'm certain that Gramps and Stan are is in my memory; there is no doubt they're fully alive there. In fact, it wouldn't surprise me in the least if this morning on the drive I heard Gramps mumbling incessantly about something and Stan hissing, "I wish he'd just shut the fuck up."

So in the jungle of my recent past, I have somehow mellowed. I don't really give a damn whether or not I see or kill an elk today. In fact, there's a small part of me that doesn't really want to get one. I didn't even bring my own Winchester rifle; I just told Dad I'd use his 721 "'cause it's a real elk killer." Truthfully, I never even shot my .30-06 to make sure it was still zeroed in for this season—and I know Dad's is. I just want to see if I can bring back those old feelings about hunting that aren't sexy—they're just wool plaid and smell like coffee.

There're certainly different levels people go through in their pursuit of activities they love. I may have *tried* to find new things I liked better than hunting, but they just never gained a hold on me. I tried boxing, which is rugged and fun, I tried guitar, which also gave me a rush, and I tried having a regular career first as a firefighter and then as a schoolteacher, but I only barely reached proficiency at firefighting and I'm still confused about teaching. I'm certain it's just because I didn't think about them as often as I did hunting deer, elk, and antelope with a rifle. So as I merged onto I-15 that morning, I realized I had reached a new level of hunting, dare I say, beyond novice? I was appreciating things beyond just barrel lengths of rifles, the double-radius shoulders of Weatherby cartridges, and how a gunshot sounds in the next canyon over. Oh yes, I still love those things, but this morning I actually noticed the stars, took a purposeful snoot full of diesel exhaust, and sipped my coffee, instead of popping a No-Doz stay-awake pill and slurping and spilling black-ass gas station coffee all over myself. I would have liked to hear "Calling Elvis" on the truck stereo, but my dad and Gail don't do music in the car for some reason, so it was just the hum of the tires, the growl of the Cummins diesel, and my dad himself perhaps starting to cross over into a new level of hunting, as he mumbled on and on like Gramps. Any minute now he might even say, "Ya can't eat tracks."

And when you reach new levels of proficiency at stuff, and think you're all worldly and shit, you start getting all kinds of new opportunities to screw up. Maybe it's like a golfer who finally starts to play a decent game, like he can shoot in the 70s. Then he'll start to get all kinds of situations where like, on a par three, his shot off the tee lands thirty feet from the pin. Now he can sink a helluva sweet putt and get a birdie or whatever, but he can also miss and get a par, or fuck up entirely and get 5 or 10 on that hole. Most likely it'll be the birdie or the par if he's truly on that new level.

So it should have been no surprise to me that because I didn't care if I got any shooting or not, that I would spot a herd of at least twenty elk trotting along the sidehill parallel to where Dad, Gail, and I were hiking within minutes of shutting down the wheelers at the bottom of the basin. I could spot them only because it looked like a giant centipede moving across the bare slope. The sound of us coming into the basin on the four-wheelers had obviously spooked them out of a lower canyon, and they were most likely headed into the timber over the top and into the next unit. Yes, it felt like I had crossed into a renaissance hunting mode as we had driven there that morning, but I was just like a little kid again when I saw those elk. I grabbed my dad's wrist and Gail's wrist simultaneously (and hard enough they probably had bruises) and hissed "Get down! There they are!"

Then what do you do? It's still too dark to take a long shot, and the herd seemed to have in mind exactly where they wanted to be. But some kind of hunting instinct kicked in or maybe it was just training and experience; or maybe it was just that I was not going to fuck around here. "You guys wait right here, I going to try and intercept them up the road."

The road of which I speak kind of switches back and forth and meanders its way toward the west end of the basin. It's a pretty mellow walk if you're in shape, not so mellow if you're 300+ pounds, which I then was. The only difference was that I was on a mission. I felt like a big fat housecat who suddenly looks pretty damn athletic and agile when it spies a robin perched on the swing-set in the back yard.

I figured I had about 200 more yards to close, or maybe two more switchbacks to conquer before I would be in shooting range. But as I rounded the bend, there they were trotting across the road. It was now or it was never. It was game on.

I had reached a point in my hunting career, or maybe in my maturity level, where the way I handled my rifle was such that I might look like an armed hiker with an old rifle now, instead of a Marine Corporal on patrol with an M-16. I used to carry my .30-06 in both hands all day long, with my right index finger just outside the trigger guard, my thumb close to the trademark Winchester three-position safety, and the rest of my fingers curled around the walnut pistol grips. My left hand was always in a place where I wouldn't have to adjust it all to provide perfect forward stability. My hands, fingers, and brain were wired for a hair trigger. Now, though, I had the rifle slung on my back, and I didn't even have a round in the chamber. Hell, it wasn't even my rifle.

But I knew what to do. I didn't have to wait for the go-ahead from the old man or anything like that. It was *barely* light enough to shoot when I went down on one knee, jacked one of my dad's hand-loaded 180-

grain Speer Grand-Slam-tipped shells into the chamber, and started sending lead downrange.

I usually get my money's worth when it comes to shooting. I would like to say that with all my "worldliness and experience" that I'm a one-shot-one-kill type of guy, but the truth is I almost always empty the magazine of my rifle at an animal once I start banging away. I either make a decent first shot and the animal runs off like it isn't even scratched (which is not uncommon with a good heart/lung hit) and I get nervous and then empty the gun, or I use the first three or four rounds to simply terrify the animal before the last bullet or two finally makes contact. I'm not proud of this fact.

It was the latter in this case. Because there was no bullet in the chamber, the magazine held four rounds. The first three got the herd galloping, the fourth took out the lead cow. It was still so dark when I was shooting that the fire coming out the end of the barrel looked just like what you see in the movies. The fourth bullet made that telltale slap/thud that is indicative of a solid hit. The elk made it about five more gallops and rolled to a stop in the snow and sagebrush just off a little knoll. That's all there was to it—I'd sunk the thirty-foot birdie putt.

We walked back down to the wheelers all kind of wondering what the hell had just happened. I had never taken an elk so easily. It was even easier getting it field-dressed and back to the truck, thanks in large part to those little Japanese horses. By 9:00 in the morning the elk was on a tarp in the garage, with me still scratching my head as to how come I got an easy one when I didn't even want one, when I'd expected to work my ass off and get nothing at all.

Such is hunting.

14—The Torch

FOR EVERY ONE EASY HUNT, there's gonna be at least ten hard ones. I know that, I'm not naïve, but I also know that the difficulty can be mitigated through the combination of attitude and physical fitness, i.e. if you're in shape and generally happy, then who fucking cares, you're alive and you're outside in the clean mountain air, and the view is the only thing that might take your breath away.

I'm no stranger to the physical misery of a good hard hunt. It's sometimes difficult for me to deal with pathological mental issues when the world becomes silent and still, but usually even these can be beaten down for the most part when you've been doing your level best to live a clean life. In 2006, I weighed 315 pounds, so if I hadn't gotten an easy cow, maybe I would've been the one getting packed off the mountain. A couple of years later, I was down to 205 pounds and fresh off completion of a marathon, a triathlon, and a stint as an amateur boxer. You are goddamn right I was ready to rock'n'roll.

But guess what will still kick your ass: frigid-ass temps and deep snow and steep hills. I don't care how fit you are, you'll still have to work at it.

Life was good, though; I was in a good place mentally, and though I didn't walk around with a dorky smile or recite the AA prayer or any of that shit,

I had an inner smile and satisfaction that I had pulled my life out of a definite nosedive — due largely to the birth of my son William.

The old man still wore plaid wool pants with wool suspenders, but he'd reached the point where he was fully satisfied to come along and still be a main character in these stories, even if he wasn't the shooter. Still my truck groaned when I started it in the morning, and still my dad's Dodge was idling in his driveway when I pulled up in my truck to move my gear to the back seat of his pickup. Maybe that's why hunting worked well in my life: because the motions involved in it are so constant, yet there's always the possibility for excitement. I like life that way. I like to operate within well-defined boundaries and under self-guidance about my circumstances, and if all the "surprises" are things I am prepared for or even expecting, then all the better. *This* is hunting.

I stretched my arms out and took in the stars and diesel exhaust and the cold. I was thankful for big Maverick mugs of scalding coffee and warm heaters, though another constant about traveling in a car with Dad is that he is never going to be satisfied with the temperature. "More heat please." "You could cut that heat down anytime you wanted." "How about opening the vents on the floor and putting that heat up a little." Sometimes, I swear to God, we have been cruising up I-15 with the heater cranked to the max and the windows down. This is hunting, though, and this was his truck and his four-wheelers, and even his rifle (the good one) on this trip, so he pretty much gets to make these decisions if he wants to.

However, one thing that is both irritating and humorous at the same time is how the old man still believes he's calling *all* the shots—it's a thing that some dads do and they never get past. Since we're talking about the consistency of things, I still get told when to gear the truck down on hills, when to put the transfer case in 4-wheel-drive, which potholes and ruts to avoid, and how to open a barbed-wire gate. It's at once endearing and at the same time, depending on my mood, infuriating. I've been going through this ritual now for the better part of twenty-five years, but you'd think I still don't know the right stuff to put in my backpack, which way is north, or that the elk tag in my pocket is for "antlerless" and that means don't shoot a bull. I'm serious. These transactions aren't unique to my dad and me, they're probably more like universal for all fathers and sons, but I am vowing to break the cycle, or at least try to water it down some. My dad will tell me where to hunt today, how long to hunt, where to glass, and when to shoot (or at least he'll think he's telling me). What he mustn't realize is that he's the one who taught me all this stuff anyway already—he may as well be talking to himself, which is maybe how fathers want it anyway.

From the truck, we head west up the dirt road on the same old four-wheelers: a dark green Honda Fourtrax and a red Honda Rancher. The Rancher has a dorky-ass windshield on it; my dad rides that one. The windshield looks dorky in town, but it sure would be nice to have right now! The green wheeler used to have one, but I think somebody has rolled this machine at some point, judging from the telltale scratches and bent handlebars, and I bet that's when the windshield was forcibly removed as well. The hardware to mount it is still attached. I follow Dad out of respect and eat all the dust.

This country is interesting. I don't think I've ever been in here in hunting season when the parking area and low country isn't dry, dusty, and relatively warm. This is a trap, though, because if you don't dress like you're gonna be in the arctic soon, you're screwed. It doesn't take but twenty minutes on the wheelers and you're in snow and arctic temperatures. It happens fast, and when it happens, you know you're in elk country.

As we motor up the road into the same basin where I took the easy cow several years ago, I look over on the same sidehill and see the same centipede of elk moving across it. You just gotta love the consistencies of life when the consistencies are cool. This time, though, we are significantly farther behind the herd, and they're going to be crossing that road up there, where I did the shooting, a lot sooner than before. And I still get excited, even though my permit is just for a cow. I gear down the green wheeler to get some punch and chew partially off the road and up the hill to get even with my dad. I gesture aggressively toward the hill, in hopes he'll understand that I see elk. He doesn't get my meaning, so he stops, and I have to say, far too loudly, "Elk."

"Where?"

"There."

This is one of those conundrums about hunting with a partner. Had I been alone, I would have kept the RPMs on the green wheeler gunned all the way through the frozen creek bed, around the hairpin turn through the dark timber, and up a couple of switchbacks. I would have intercepted the herd in exactly the same spot as before, when they trotted across the road just like they had before. The difference this time is that instead of walking, I would've been on the wheeler, the elk would have been more spooked because of that, so they'd have been galloping, and it would have been a more "assholes and elbows" situation—something which I'm not entirely fond of but am perfectly capable of handling.

Either way, it didn't matter, because by the time I explained to my dad what we should do and then patiently waited while he explained to me what we should do, using words identical to those I had just spoken, the elk had gained too much ground. So we putted farther up the road into the basin and I regained my composure about why I was here in the first place. Hunting is so much more than killing; it's just that it *is* hard to pass up easy ones. When the easy ones cross the road and get out of range, before you even have your rifle out of its case, it's time to switch your brain from sprint mode to marathon mode. This was not going to be a duck shoot; it was going to be an elk hunt.

We parked and shut down the wheelers at a wide spot in the two-track and sat for a second. This silent moment is another standard and profound part of hunting. When you shut your truck or four-wheeler engine off, you're crossing from a modern day hunter back in time to the really old days, if only just for a moment. Yes, you can still hear little ticks and clicks from the engine cooling off, but basically it's silent. Very silent. So silent it can be unnerving. Now you will walk and listen and look. Now you may have to be cold or maybe cold and sweating at the same time. If only just for the moment you might feel the gravity of your place in the world as a predator, and more than just some redneck wasting time on a Saturday. In the sky above you there's either so much space and time, and so many stars that you might feel disturbingly unimportant in the scheme of things; or there's wind and clouds and maybe even snow. For the latter, you just zip up, tighten down, and cowboy up. For the former, you try to just roll with it, and accept what is and what isn't.

Maybe I'm the only one who thinks this way. It's sure hard to understand if Dad does, as he works to get ready faster than I do, and indeed is ready to hike while I'm still trying to zip my pants up after taking a pee and staring up at the stars trying to find the Big Dipper. He hands me his rifle, the 721. He won't even let me put it on the four-wheeler I'm driving; that rifle is his baby. Soon we've hiked through the lowest patch of timber and we're working our way out of the switchbacks. I'm going slow because I like to try to see elk before they see me — funny thing about them, you'll usually see a deer before you hear it, and you'll usually hear an elk before you see it. I'm also walking slowly because I care more about staying at the old man's speed and hanging out with him than I do about proving to myself what daily swim, bike, and run training will do to help cardiovascular fitness. I think I could jog to the top of this basin without stopping even once.

It's daylight now, and I do see the same herd of elk I saw centipeding across the slope earlier. They're making their way (again looking like a centipede) over the top through kind of a couloir at the back of the basin. They've already crossed through the shooting gallery and now they're probably a thousand yards away, so I'm not grabbing anyone's wrists or jacking rounds into the chamber or metaphorically shitting my pants. I'm simply checking them out; I don't even know, or care, whether Dad has seen them. I know exactly where they're headed and what they'll do when they get there. I store this in my brain. The very last thing I see is an impressive 6-point bull at the back of the herd as he crests the ridge. Damn, it's fun to see big bull elk, even if that's not your legal prey for the day.

After those few switchbacks that take you through the shooting gallery, the road leads into a saddle. In the past, this has been both a geographical transition point, where you can see almost all of this beautiful basin as well as most of the adjacent drainage to the north, and also an activity transition point, as it represents the place where you decide what you're gonna do for the day (assuming you didn't get an easy cow). When I stop to look around and soak in the morning sun, I can see at least three more groups of elk, along with a small band of mule deer. It *is* a beautiful day, weather and mountain scenery alone, not to mention the proximity of legal game. The closest elk are probably a thousand yards away, but seem to be unconcerned about our presence here in the saddle. That makes us all content, because I'm not overly concerned about their presence either.

I decide to continue on through the saddle and look over the other side, just in case there's any elk in here close—you don't ever pass up an easy one. I don't see any, but the sun sure feels good, so I decide to sit and wait for Dad to catch up. Yet another partner-hunting conundrum: if you try to be a decent person in life, you'll gauge the other guy's attitude about the day and factor that into your plans, especially when that other guy is your 73-year-old father. So I think I'll let him make the call, and of course he does. "Why don't you keep going up a little farther there, see if there's any elk around the corner. I'll go back down where we just were and watch those elk way over there. Maybe we can work something on them."

"Okay."

I move on along the road for another quarter-mile or so. It's such a nice day that I don't mind just strolling along here, rifle slung on my back, looking at this awesome country. I don't even have binocs with me today, I'm just soaking it all in. Then something suddenly comes over me. Almost instantly my ambition and my prey drive and my something-I-don't-know-what like my previous "aggressive me" all take over.

Instead of continuing on down the road, I turn abruptly to my left and start post-holing it through the thigh-deep snow straight up the mountain. I know where that first herd of elk is, and I'm going to go get one of them. I'm certain they continued over the top and they're going to be bedded down somewhere over on the west slope, almost over on the Birch Creek side. I know if I don't just buckle down and put to use this sudden onset of physical and mental intensity that has lain dormant within me for at least ten years, I'm going to regret it. I'm going to regret it because my dad will persuade me to make a cockamamie stalk on the other elk he went back to look at with his binocs. It's cockamamie mainly because it won't be my idea, and it's simply ridiculous that I might still be talked into going after elk that I don't want to. It's a symbol of a greater thing in life between fathers and sons that can be explained by something much less complicated: I simply cannot take orders from the back seat anymore when I'm driving. I love the guy, but I generally have a good idea what I need to do next. He may not accept it yet, but the hunting torch has been passed, and this particular torch holds four 180-grain bullets in the magazine.

My motor is just humming as I buck the drifts of crusted-over snow that have accumulated on the north side of this slope. I step on it, it holds for a half-second, and then I bust through it and sink, over and over again, all the while moving straight up a steep slope. I don't feel guilty about leaving the old man to look over the basin and sit in the sunshine. In fact, if I were my son, I would want my son to be doing this. I would want him to feel alive again, and acting independent, like a man. I would want him to be putting to use all the literal blood, sweat, and tears from the last two decades into a late-season cow elk hunt. This is our favorite family pastime; why not uphold that tradition in real style?

An hour later I'm over the top and looking at the very same herd of elk from early this morning. They're all over the bare sidehill doing their thing; some are pawing at the snow, some of them are meandering around, and a few are already bedded. It's around 10:00 in the morning. Between them and me is nothing, no cover. There are no trees, no gullies, no rocks; just about 800 yards of space. The 721 is a good shooter, and I can handle it well, but it's not a $12,000 CheyTac sniper rifle. I've got to get closer, but I don't know how.

I can also see those two other herds that my dad is probably watching. I am sitting on an imaginary dividing line between those two herds and this herd. It's "six of one, a half-dozen of the other." So I do something unthinkable. I simply stand up and start walking down that dividing line between the herds. It's actually slightly more than imaginary because there is an old two-track road. I'm just going to walk straight over to the bare sidehill and then go right or left, depending on which herd of elk stays put.

As I get closer and closer to the hill, I can see some of the elk that were previously bedded start to stand up. Most of the elk are more than occasionally looking at me. They know I'm out of place, but maybe if elk think intuitively, they are thinking that no hunter is stupid enough to just walk right straight-up out in the open like that, so therefore we must be safe. I decide to concentrate on the herd to my right, the original ones, the ones I saw going through the couloir, the ones my dad isn't looking at, the ones my dad would suggest *against* going after. It feels like I have to do this just to prove a point to myself.

But none of the elk run off. They stay right there, and I have now made it to the same sidehill that they're on, only now I'm out of sight again. *Holy shit, they never ran*, I'm thinking.

Now I'm past the point of all my mental shit-talking; I've actually gotta start moving quietly and slowly. It's not a mental pissing match between the old Ben, the new Ben, and my dad—it's an elk hunt in November below Heart Mountain.

I *know* how to do this.

The snow has accumulated in a weird way across this hill and out on the flat areas leading into the timber on the Birch Creek side. In many places, there's none, in other places, big drifts, and where I'm going to do my stalk, it's about knee deep. The situation is much like Charlie Brown and the bitch with the football. Every step you take, the snow says, "Go

179

ahead, put your weight on that foot, I can hold you."
And it does, for a second or two, and then it gives and
you fall through, over and over again. This makes it
tricky to pull off a stalk, but it's nothing that slowing
down can't cure. It's maybe 11:00 now, took me about
an hour to get over here. I continue on around the hill
until, oops, there's some ears! *Hold still now, then slowly
go down to your knees out of sight.*

My mental instructions to myself continue, as if my
dad, Tom, Stan, and Gramps are all watching it play
out on a closed circuit TV. Their voices become one,
and it channels through the voice of my conscious
talking to me. "Drop your backpack now, and put a
round in the chamber because you're gonna be
shooting soon." Done. "Now you're gonna have to
walk in a crouch, or maybe on your knees, or even
crawl." Okay. "Focus and remember to relax and don't
make any quick movements." You got it.

At first there were four ears that were rotating like
radar trying to determine if there was a threat. Now
there are no ears. Those two elk must have moved
toward the timber. I don't move but maybe five more
steps, though, when I suddenly see my prey. It's a cow
and she's bedded and looking west, down the slope
into the timber. The snow is so loud though, that when
I move closer, her ears swivel like radar as well. She
knows something is up, especially since not too long
ago she saw a man-creature just walking right out in
the open. Something is not right; something wicked
this way comes.

Now the cow is looking right at me. I'm only about a hundred yards away, and I could probably take this head shot, but by now in my life I've finally learned that it would be better to jump the elk and never get a shot than to take a lousy shot, and miss or wound the animal. It's like playing that game you played as a kid, the red light/green light. A person would say "green light" and turn his back to you. You would get as close to the finish line as you could before the person would say "red light" and turn around. If you were still moving when he turned around, you were caught and had to go back to the start. If you just stood still, you were safe until the next green light.

Now I get the cow's green light and cover about five more yards. Red light. Green light. Five more yards. The cow has had enough and stands up. It is now or never. I actually have the presence of mind to ask myself one more time, "You sure you want to do this? Probably gonna be a bitch of a pack-out."

Fuck it. Crack! Thump!

At 75 yards, you can see the bullet hit, hear the bullet hit, and see the blood right behind the shoulder where contact was made. I am so certain it's a kill shot that I just calmly sit back for a second, roll onto one knee, then stand up and go back to retrieve my backpack. I do chamber another round, but I'm really 99.9 percent sure that I'm not going to need another. The empty shell I leave right where I jacked it out, of course; there for my kids and then for ages, I hope.

It's not hard to find the abstract-art blood trail, like Jackson Pollock came through on the back of a wild camel with a bucket of red paint. And thankfully, for my peace of mind, the cow didn't make it but maybe fifty yards. At sprint speed, that means she was in pain for maybe four seconds. Now the cow elk is a load of work that will be our winter meat, currently piled up in the snow against a small sapling.

It used to be that when one of us had a confirmed kill, we'd fire off two quick shots, letting the other guy(s) know. I don't want to do that to my dad, though, not today. I'm worried he'll try to make his way through this shit-field of snow to help me out, and there's really no need for that. I'm just hoping he heard my one shot and figures I got some action, so as not to get concerned.

This is the third animal I've field-dressed this year, so I'm not at all rusty; but geeze, elk are *big* animals. Damn, though, I feel strong, and as I grab hold of the right hind leg and with one hand yank the elk into position, I get down to business. Quickly. And happily. It's a beautiful day up here in the hills—and it's still morning.

By 1:00 that afternoon I was walking up to my dad, who was lying on his side in a patch of short brush just uphill of the basin we'd ridden earlier in the day. As I approached him, he pointed over toward one of the other groups of elk from the morning, quite a few of which were still feeding right out in the open on the same sidehill, and which were coincidentally the same group of elk I might have gone after if *my* herd had spooked.

"They're still there," he whispered. Like I hadn't noticed or couldn't see them.

"Oh, I got one," I said, trying hard to sound just as nonchalant and unexcited and casual as possible.

"You did?"

He was trying hard to sound unsurprised.

So I told him the story and we (he) decided it would be best if we came back the next day to pack the elk out.

"How many times did you have to shoot it?"

"Once."

"Hmm."

15—The Torch, Part 2

ALL WAS STILL AND SILENT. No wind, no talking; only eyes and ears and anticipation. They must have waited for what seemed like an eternity for a sharp crack, followed by the telltale thud, followed by high-fives and yee-haws. At least that's what they expected at this stage in the hunt. It's what I always talked about; it's what you see on hunting TV; it's the heretofore, to them, mysterious last step before the camera and the smiles. I knew this was what they were waiting for, but I wasn't sure I could give it to them today. I might not be able to deliver.

I am a hunter. I prefer to hunt elk over other North American game, and I prefer to eat it over any other meat. But that means I inevitably have to kill one, knowing on an ironic plane and pragmatic level that the best thing I can do for elk, as a species, is to legally kill one. I took the hunter safety course years ago, I buy a tag for at least one state every year, and I always put in for available special permit draws in Idaho. I live for the moment of excitement when I have an elk in the crosshairs of my .30-06, or my .270 Winchester, or one of my 7mm Remington Magnums, or my .300 Winchester Magnum, or my .338 Winchester Magnum, or my .340 Weatherby Magnum. This moment in time, when all else in my world is suspended, represents the ultimate nexus of hard work and luck. To me, there are few other things quite as cool as that moment. I rather doubt the elk I'm shooting at feels the same way, but that's something I'll consider only after the echoes of rifle reports have quit bouncing off the canyon walls or have dissipated across the prairie. At that point, I always have that weird mix of euphoria and remorse that only the human hunter might have.

I am a teacher. My classroom is the wild places where I take people I care about, and who want to learn about this stuff. This classroom is usually federal land that has some combination of mountains, streams, trees, and sagebrush beneath a wide blue sky. My natural resource lessons are varied — I try to show them the effects of erosion, I show them how fires can create beneficial mosaic patterns in the vegetation, and because I am also a hunter, I teach them how and why we hunt. First there were just pictures I showed them, hides and horns they could handle, and elk burgers they could chow down on. Then the time came when they could start accompanying me on hunts.

My son William's first exposure to this was on an antelope hunt. It was a perfect introductory hunt — not too cold, a walk that was not too long, and a wait of not too long before the herd of antelope walked by at a hundred yards. I downed the lead buck with a single shot from my .257 Weatherby Magnum. The little boy seemed totally hooked; it was so exciting. I still get bad buck fever and I still get visibly nervous, and it really rubs off on him. Though I still taught the boy proper respect for the animal, I will admit that smiles and high-fives displaced conservation conversation for the balance of that day. The natural high of the whole thing took a while to wear off, though I think he was mildly confused about the whole affair; he was only four years old. There were other times we returned home empty-handed, a great lesson about hunting being hunting and not necessarily killing.

Sam and Juliana's first hunt was in Unit 50, and it was cold, wet, and miserable. At that time, of my two boys and my wife, one expected a hunt to end in harvest, two were still waiting and wondering what that would be like. The lesson was not quite complete: two thought hunting was hiking, one thought hunting was killing.

I am university trained in wildlife resource management. What this means is that I know scientifically why we hunt, and I know that hunting is much more than a value-driven activity. Hunting is a sound, viable, and necessary wildlife management tool. I think I could make a reasonably educated guess about what would happen to our deer, elk, and antelope if we didn't hunt them.

I am a son. One of my favorite people on this planet is my mother, and she has made no secret of her love for me in the thirty-five years I've been alive. I can't imagine how hard it would be for me to lose her; I do know how hard it was for her to lose a son, and I can't imagine how quickly that would crush me as a father.

All of these themes converged at once in the crosshairs of my Leupold scope one late November afternoon — specifically, the last day of the late cow season in my Idaho unit. Why do so many difficult decisions arise on the last day of the season? The too-long shot at the giant bull, the bull right there in front of you being smaller than one you were holding out for, the steep and dangerous canyon full of cliffs and drop-offs where you're almost certain your bull is hiding, but you're not certain you could pack one out of there anyway. All these last-day decisions. Mine came on this day in the form of a lone cow and her calf bedded in the sagebrush 200 yards out in front of us on a small knoll. Time was 4 p.m. I don't think they even knew we were there; they didn't appear alarmed. A minute ago we hadn't known they were there either; it was a chance meeting. In fact, in my mind I had more or less closed the book on this season.

Reflexively, I dropped to one knee and my wife and boys immediately did the same. Relaxing then into a seated position, I found I had a good rifle rest. My crosshairs moved back and forth, cow to calf. Scientifically speaking, a good solid shot on the cow was the best bet. Barring other circumstances, I was fairly certain the calf would rejoin a herd and survive the winter just fine. But then I made fatal emotional mistake number one: I recalled in that instant another hunt on which I had shot a big cow elk, only to have her calf hang around about fifty yards away as I field-dressed its mama. I wondered if the calf was sad. This is anthropomorphism, I know, and I try to discourage it in these situations. *This is not Bambi.* Yet I was having second thoughts about taking the shot. That's when I moved the crosshairs over and settled them behind the calf's shoulder. A calf, I knew, would be really good eating. *Really* good. Also easy to pack out. And the cow would just head for the high country after I shot.

Couldn't do it.

My younger boy whispered, "Shoot her, Dad. What're you waiting for?" My older son and my wife didn't know what to think or what to whisper.

I put the crosshairs back on the cow. Everything in the world was contained within the sight picture of the scope. All existence faded and everything was perfectly silent. I clicked the safety off, took a deep breath, let half of it out, and began to put pressure on the trigger. Then the calf's face appeared in the left side of the picture as he nuzzled his mother's back leg. I let the breath all the way out, put the safety back on, and realized I was beginning to feel sick to my stomach. I made fatal emotional mistake number two: I thought of my own mother and how much I loved her. Anthropomorphism again. Couldn't do it.

Lowering the rifle, I decided to watch the elk for a minute. At this point, there was probably still a half hour of shooting light remaining. My choices were limited here, and influenced by a confusing jumble of emotional, physical, and mental issues. I had either animal dead-to-rights. An easy shot. Why, I asked myself, would this not even be an issue if these two animals were amongst at least a few other elk? Both boys and my wife, I knew, would certainly take away a big lesson here. Show "weakness," let both elk live and this might send what I consider an inappropriate anthropomorphic lesson to the boys. Sure, I think my dog will go to heaven, but an elk? Shoot the cow and

I've gone against that pulsating emotional drive in my brain. Plus, I do want demonstrate respect for life, and that you can't just kill things to satisfy bloodlust. I had definitely ruled out shooting the calf at this point.

Maybe I could just punt. Purposely shoot and miss. Aim way over them and put a round harmlessly into the hillside. The problem with that: the shot was way too easy and there would be time for multiple shots and maybe even a reload. These elk were a long way from cover, I bragged to my family all the time how well I could shoot, and I spend a lot of our money on rifles, scopes, and ammo.

I suppose this is as good a time as any to also mention that after five outings to fill this tag, this is the first time we had been within range of *any* elk. I am not too proud to admit that my frustration at coming home empty-handed had been building. Again, I took aim at the cow.

Looking back now, I guess I probably should have done what my permit said I should have done: made a clean shot on the cow and benefitted the herd as a whole. Alternatively, I wish I could have just said to my family, "I'm just feeling too soft-hearted today to shoot either one. It would make me sad."

Instead, I made a feeble and shanked punt. I just told them it was getting too dark and that we should just let them go and continue on our way back to the truck. They knew it was weak, I knew it was weak. It probably confused them. I'm still confused. What if this happens again?

My dad hadn't passed the torch to me in such a confusing manner. It seemed he had always known the proper sequence of the lesson so as to hand off to me a burning desire to continue the family's tradition. I don't think I was born to love to hunt. My dad showed it to me in a way that instilled love for mountains and animals and rifles; and how they all fit into this brutal but beautiful cycle.

With my stepson Sam in Unit 50

I am also a marathon runner, or I should say, I once ran a marathon. That particular experience taught me, in a very physical and solid lesson, that nothing good comes easy; the finish line is so far away that you may as well enjoy every step you take until you cross that finish line. At the finish line of the marathon, because I had run the marathon so slowly, there weren't even many people there; they'd gone home. I had expected all sorts of pomp and circumstance; instead there was just a dude with a microphone standing on the sidewalk, and he called out my time on the microphone and handed me a finisher's medal. It was drizzling rain. Over on another part of the sidewalk were a couple crates of pint-sized cartons of chocolate milk. Nothing else. It was kind of anticlimactic and vague. I guess that's how I'll have to pass the torch in this new day and age of hunting. I won't be able to show it off like it's an algebra lesson. I'll have to be more literary and artistic and spiritual about it. I just hope they can love it like I do, and realize that the finish line of killing an animal is sometimes kind of anticlimactic and vague.

16—His and Hers Antelope

SOMEONE CALCULATED ONE TIME how much the average cost per pound of venison might be if you considered the production costs related to it. These are just some of those costs: ammo, tags, backpacks, boots, clothes, fuel, licenses, and packaging/processing. If you took a deer every other year, it would come to about $30 a pound, and I doubt that includes $1000 rifles and scopes. If you're considering hunting based on grocery economics, remember that $30 per pound estimate. The idea that you'll save money by hunting for your meat instead of buying beef at the store is a very weak argument.

I had a good idea about what it costs to hunt going into my marriage, and my wife surely isn't naïve to those costs. In those first few years of marriage, remember, hunting was *sexy*. But when I asked if I could buy a new rifle "because that old .30-06 of mine is gettin' worn out, and the .300 Win Mag is too powerful for deer," her attitude kind of soured. The Unit 50 trail of misery hunt I had taken her and Sam on didn't help matters; and then there was the cow and calf drama. And then I went deer hunting on opening day in Unit 58 with my dad, and we saw eight does and no less than fifty hunters! No bullshit, I sat on a rock outcrop and counted them roaming around the valley below me on foot, horseback, four-wheeler, and pickup (and these were the easy ones to see, wearing blaze orange clothing). I started to kind of get sour about it myself, at least as far as the general seasons go around my hometown of Idaho Falls. It just started to wear on me—and my budget—so I told myself and my wife that I wasn't going to go hunting in Idaho again unless I drew a special permit. A special permit in Idaho means you draw a special experience, far removed from the idea of competing with the crackers to have a small chance at a deer or elk in the short rifle seasons. Don't get me wrong—with time, good boots, a high level of motivation and physical fitness (or horses), you can escape the general masses of yayhoos that run around on four-wheelers and try to use elk bugles to call elk with their four-wheeler still running (I did witness that one time).

And six years passed with no special permit drawn. I started to get pretty pissy about it. Every year I would put in my application in May, and every July I would check the internet and get the message "Sorry. This license was not drawn for any special permits" or something like that. Then my wife, whose favorite hobby is culinary arts—she's a food blogger at JuliesJazz.com—happened to read a book called *Girl Hunter: Revolutionizing the Way We Eat, One Hunt at a Time* by Georgia Pellegrini. If there are any parallels in your life with hunting and with the culinary arts, you will read this book eventually. For my wife, the main thing is cooking, but she's a traditionalist and wants to know where her food comes from. Since 2003, she has lived in a house that often smells like gun solvent; she

194

has to look at a rack full of dusty guns on the bedroom wall every day. There may not have actually been parallels there, but the opportunity to test the waters of "knowing where your food comes from" has always been available. "Next fall I want to get my hunting license and go hunting with you," she said. Thank you, Georgia Pellegrini.

In reality, it was more than that. It was me wanting to share things I like to do with my family. "That deer hunt we went on was totally extraordinary," I told her. "It usually isn't that tough." And it was also Juliana wanting to participate and be a good sport in things I like to do. I usually return the favor: I have taken yoga and aerobics classes and read a book about Gelsey Kirkland, I watch "Chopped" on the Food Network, and I know about Ree Drummond and Bobby Flay. I even sometimes drink tea!

So Juliana dutifully took the Idaho hunter safety course, passed the written and practical exams, and even told me she found the information pretty interesting (it's a lot more than just firearm safety). The next step was the hunting license, and the third was applying for the special permits. And you guessed it: call it beginner's luck, or maybe Idaho Fish and Game know that we need more women and kids out there big-game hunting, but on her first application for an antelope hunt, she drew it. Haha, what's even better is that my name was attached to hers on a party hunt, so when she drew, I drew. In September there was going to be a "his and hers" antelope hunt in the Birch Creek Valley.

Because I can't separate the thoughts of big-game hunting and high-powered rifles (it's like trying to think about Communion only as bread and not wine, or Dallas and not Cowboys), my *very* first order of business was setting us up with rifles. Every time you draw a special permit, you have to get a new gun. That is just God's law for American firearm hunters. It doesn't even have to be the one you're going to use on the hunt, maybe just in the ballpark; e.g. after I drew one of those cow elk hunts, I bought a Smith and Wesson Model 686 .357 Magnum. Because Juliana had drawn an antelope tag too, *she* now needed a rifle.

I love caliber arguments; they are *the only thing* I would ever debate about all day long with another person. I don't even care if I'm right, I just love talking about and thinking about and arguing about what is the best gun for this species overall, what is the best gun for this species in this hunting situation or that situation, what is the best caliber for that gun, what action works best, and on and on and on. In high school, a girl I had a crush on was telling me about a deer hunt her dad took her on. She ended up getting a damn nice muley, but when I asked her what kind of rifle she used, she replied, "I don't know, a brown one." I had to lose my crush on her.

Juliana works at a place where probably 95 percent of the people are hunters. Because she's a blogger and people know what she's up to, I didn't want her to be the girl who responded, when asked what kind of gun she would use for her antelope hunt, "I don't know, it has a scope on it. And it's brown." This would reflect poorly on me! We had to do some work. We watched hunting videos, she read hunting magazines, she talked to people at work, and in the end she bought what I knew we were going to buy the whole time: a .243 Winchester. Yep, it is the best caliber in the history of the nation for small-statured women, younger kids, and first-time hunters. And dandy for antelope. Woo-hoo!

The .243 Winchester is based on the .308 Winchester cartridge, which is a favorite of snipers. The .308 (with a bullet diameter of 308 thousandths of an inch) shell casing is "necked down" to fit the smaller caliber .243 bullet. The smaller bullet has a higher velocity than the .308, which may not make it the best caliber for elk perhaps, but technically this means it would have less recoil (it's all about Newton's laws). But as my brother once said, "It's all shot placement," and at the end of the day, you've just got to pick a gun that you can shoot well. Applying that statement to what I think would work for Juliana, she doesn't need a gun that's going to kick. Really, who wants to argue that there is better caliber than a .243 Winchester for a woman's first antelope hunt? This will be *her* rifle.

And because I'm making proclamations now, who would like to dispute the fact that the .257 Weatherby Magnum is the God-given cartridge for antelope, the best there is for this species? That has to be *my* rifle. I would've suggested we both get those, but the .257 Weatherby is a belted-magnum cartridge, so it has significantly more recoil than a .243 — and it's a lot louder.

I also drew a bull elk tag for the season. So we needed a total of three new rifles. Sonofabitch, I thought when I realized this, it's a good *and* bad day. Good because we're shopping for guns. Bad because, well, we're shopping for guns, and it's almost like buying a car. It seems like it takes all day long, and I've never had money saved for a gun, so this is accomplished via Visa. Days that are bad *and* good end with you feeling like you're walking on cloud nine with a stomachache. Yep, we were now the proud new owners of a Weatherby Vanguard S2 .257 Weatherby Magnum, a Weatherby Vanguard S2 .338 Winchester Magnum, and a Remington Model 700 SPS .243 Winchester — and some more debt.

The hunt opened on Wednesday, September 20, and what a beautiful morning it was! There was not a hint of wind, and the Toyota didn't even groan when I fired it up. The first stop: Maverick, to get a couple of those gas station coffees my wife and I love, more for tradition than taste, for our way out of town on the highway. Ironically, we didn't talk too much about hunting on the hour-and-a-half drive, and that may be because it was the first time we had left town, just the two of us, in nearly four years. There is a lot of conversation that has to be taken care of when you don't have the interruption of an attention-seeking little boy in the back seat.

198

There are three turns I miss every time I drive into this country in the dark, whether it's to hunt deer or antelope. The first is the turn off the highway. Yep, missed it. The next is the right fork after the first gate. Again, missed it. Both screw-ups took u-turns to correct, which took time, which started to get my panties in a wad. I don't know whether I was showing it or not, but I consider showing up late to the trailhead or parking spot a cardinal sin when hunting. Whenever my dad would make wrong turns or when one of us caused us to be late, my dad would start whistling little tunes that weren't really tunes. If my dad was behind the wheel and whistling little pointless tunes, you knew you were dealing with human nitroglycerin at that point, and it was best to avoid becoming the blasting cap. My wife won't put up with that shit, so I just started getting sweaty and looking out the window into the darkness as if I could actually see something.

I finally had to pull out the GPS. (I know myself enough to know I need to make brain backups so as not to get lost out here on the prairie.) I managed to get us to the parking spot, but fifteen or twenty minutes late, and by the time we were through fucking around with backpacks and rifles it was breaking daylight.

Shit! We took about ten steps from the truck and I could just barely see the white shape of an antelope walking across the prairie ahead of us. "Get down," I hissed, "there's one right there!"

With the scope I could see it was a doe, and though she wasn't running, she was moving with a purpose —

I'm sure she knew we were there. However, this was opening day of the rifle season, so our mere presence wasn't cause for terror yet. Juliana and I had either-sex tags, though, and Juliana had said that if she got an easy shot at a doe, she was going to take it. I had at this point forgotten all those deeper meanings about why I hunt. I was 100 percent in the here and now, and this situation was pissing me off because it wasn't what I had planned. My plan was to have made it over to the pass where we always got shooting, set up a nice little machine-gun nest, and wait for an ambush.

It was close enough to legal shooting time that, theoretically, one of us could have taken the shot. On one hand, how cool would that be, shooting within minutes of the opening day? On the other hand, how sad would that be to have half our tags filled within minutes of the dawn of opening day? The doe moved on out of range before Juliana could get set up, which I was glad for, because the rest of the day was so much more interesting than that shot would have been.

We moved together across the prairie toward the ambush spot, at that time of the morning when there's just a splash of sunlight in the eastern sky and you can still see maybe just a few stars in the western part of the sky. I love it. You can hear cars down on the highway, and I always wonder why all those people aren't up here antelope hunting right now. What could be more important? I suppose they're headed to work or school, but I hope they have wishes to be out here in the stillness on the prairie. I have those wishes when I'm in the middle of boredom or some kind of shitstorm. I wish I was out hunting, or on a beach, or on a plane to Las Vegas, or on a road trip to Boise in the spring.

It was hard to guess how Juliana was feeling at this point. But I'd say she was more into the moment than I was, and nervous enough because we'd already spotted legal game. It was how I had been feeling moments before when we saw that first doe.

Then we skirted a little knoll and dammit, right back to all business! Here came a doe and a little buck cresting the very ridge we were supposed to have crossed thirty minutes ago. "Get down, there they are!" I hissed again.

I was sounding altogether too aggressive, and I think that's just because I wanted Juliana to have the best chance possible. And what's this business about "getting down"? I suppose it's because if an antelope (or deer or elk) sees a human walking straight-up, there's no doubt it's a human and it's time to bug out; but if said human is crouched down, even in plain sight, maybe the animal will doubt itself, and sometimes that moment of doubt can be fatal. I think I was being a little too focused, though — kind of like when I was in my 20s — and it rattled Juliana.

I threw my pack down in front of her and tried to be calm. "Lay your rifle across my pack. The one in back is a buck. Shoot him."

The antelope were seemingly unaware of our presence and continued on a more or less straight walk past us at less than 100 yards. There was barely even any sagebrush. It was like they were committing suicide. Juliana seemed to have her .243 trained on them. I waited a few feet behind and to her right. I waited for a BANG to break the stillness. Nothing. Nothing. And so I turned into my dad.

"What the hell's the matter? Take him. Why aren't you shooting? What's going on?" All this was hissed as pleasantly as I could, but I was probably bleeding the fun out of it a little.

The antelope passed innocently over the little knoll and continued their purposeful walk south, right to where we had just been. In fact, it looked like they were headed for the parked Toyota. As soon as they were out of sight, I hissed at Juliana again. "Let's go, maybe we can get a shot from on top of that knoll."

I stood up and started moving out. "What about the backpack?" she asked.

"Just leave the fuckin' thing there! We'll be back in a second."

"But my camera's in there."

"Dammit, nobody's gonna steal your camera out here on the prairie."

It was a good thing I'd become somewhat more introspective with age; not that my wife would have put up with too much more of that shit. I relented. "Sorry babe, it's just that I get all nervous and stuff, you know. It's no big deal, you'll get another chance; just probably not one quite as easy." I don't know why I had to get that last dig in there. I could tell she felt a little dejected on one hand, but excited on the other. Here it was barely breaking day and we'd already seen three antelope.

The next time we saw the doe and the little buck they were clear south of the Toyota, so we continued on to "antelope pass" to sit in the little outcrop of rocks where I had planned to be in the first place. When we got there, I made a little gunners' turret for us and then we hid and looked over the prairie in silence. The weather forecast had called for wind and snow and rain, but all we could see was blue sky with a few wispy clouds. It was windless and actually comfortable. I propped my .257 Weatherby against a rock, acting more like the guide now, while Juliana held her .243 across her lap.

It hadn't been five minutes when she hunter-hissed, "There's one!" As she was saying it, I caught movement out of the corner of my left eye. God I love that feeling! It's what antelope pass is all about—stillness and silence and then the shit hits the fan. But when I put both eyes on the movement, I saw that it was just a coyote. Still, the rush is awesome!

Then we went back to the other half of the reason we were there, and that was just looking and thinking. Here on the prairie you get to lay out all your thoughts and examine them to see which ones you want to analyze a little more. I thought first of rifles, which I always do when I'm hunting—and that leads to reminiscing about the old days. I thought of the BLM and how we used to run around this country putting out fires. I thought about past party days and how my life had so drastically changed for the better since I'd quit drinking. I thought about how lucky I was to have my wife and my boys. I would like to know what

Juliana was thinking. Was she still all keyed up, like when I first started hunting? Were all her thoughts focused on the here and now? How long without seeing any game would it be before she started getting bored? And then movement out of the corner of my right eye jolted me back to the present. "There they are!" I hissed at her.

But, again, my excitement had led me to speak too soon. It was a group of mule deer making their way on a perpendicular course through antelope pass. A 3-point buck followed two does and what looked like a fawn. They passed within fifty yards of us and never knew we were there.

And then came the rain.

What the hell? It was beautiful just a few minutes ago! I don't care about shitty weather when I'm hunting alone or with my dad, but this is my wife here, it's supposed to be a nice day! Can't you see she needs to have nice weather so she'll like hunting so I can continue to hunt and buy guns! Come on world— throw me a bone here! And the droplets turned from drizzle to snow to driving rain to driving snow to horizontal sleet to a damn mess. I covered Juliana in a tarp and told her, "I bet this'll pass here pretty soon." She hung on gamely, but I happen to know that she not only dislikes situations like this, they actually piss her off.

Finally I exercised some judgment and said, "Okay, if it doesn't clear up in thirty minutes we'll head back to the truck."

204

Thirty more minutes and a thirty-minute walk and we were back in the truck with the heater roaring, drinking hot coffee. I hated to admit it, but it was kind of pleasant. That is, until I looked over on the ridge where we had just walked and spotted a dozen antelope there. The only way they could have gotten there is to come through antelope pass. "Don't get upset, okay?" Juliana said, before I even said anything. "Well, that's hunting," I replied, conceding defeat for the moment.

My new plan was to get out of sight as quickly as possible, and anyone who's hunted antelope will agree with me that generally they won't spook if your vehicle is moving, it's when you stop that they get nervous. We cut northeast, away from the spot where we'd parked, and headed for a two-track road that would put us even with, but about 600 yards below, antelope pass. When we came back into sight of them again, I could see that my plan was working, as the small herd was now just kind of grazing and meandering back north right through antelope pass again. Sometimes you have to have a little patience. I said, "Let's wait in the truck here for a few minutes and as soon as they're out of sight, we'll try to move in on them."

Typical of Idaho in September, the weather had changed on a dime by now, and it was just partly cloudy, no rain or anything, so when the antelope fed out of sight behind another little ridge, we grabbed our rifles and bailed. No coats, packs, nothing. Just rifles.

How many times have you made this mistake in your hunting life?

Being in pretty good shape, Juliana and I covered the distance quickly, and just as I had predicted, the herd was still just moseying along as we came over a little rise. "Okay, down," I whispered, much calmer than I had been earlier in the day.

Now it was time for the good old-fashioned duck-walk-knee-crawl into position. Juliana later said it was hard for her to be serious and keep a straight face, and not think about Elmer Fudd saying "Shhh. Be vewy, vewy quiet; I'm hunting wabbits."

If I had known she was thinking that then, I might have had serious misgivings about this myself, because it does seem kind of juvenile, in a way, this whole hunting business. But on the contrary, I was as focused as a housecat on a yard mouse. The setup was perfect: less than a hundred yards, antelope didn't know we were there, Juliana and her .243 propped over a rock, all outdoor channel TV.

Antelope must have a sixth sense, or maybe it's just their eyesight that's about eight times as powerful as a human's, but suddenly they were running. Shooting at a running antelope is about as far from ideal as you can get, and Juliana knew it, so I did not expect her to shoot. I just couldn't take it anymore though.

"Do you care if I take a shot?" I whispered. "No, go for it!" she urged.

The last antelope was about a 12-inch buck. Ka-BANG!! The .257 Weatherby Mag is a prairie-silence shatterer, and though I had aimed ahead of the

206

running animal, he seemed to have made it over the hill unscathed. Still, we got up, shrugged at each other, and went over to about where he had been when I shot; we looked for a blood trail for a while. Fifteen minutes or so later, I looked through my binocs across the flats and there they were looking back at us, at least a half mile away. I could still see the buck with them. "Oh well," I thought, and shrugged to myself. At least I'd broken the shot-free silence.

"Well, I guess that's it for now. Let's head back down to the truck," I suggested.

The way Juliana was walking I could tell that she was not really digging this too much. I knew she knew it was probably going to be a long rest of the day, doing this type of thing over and over again, and then finally just going home empty-handed. She had the .243 slung on her back and was looking at the ground while she walked.

"What are you thinking about?" I asked.

And as she thought about how she was going to respond to that and not hurt my feelings by saying hunting is just kind of stupid, the hunting gods threw us another bone, proving once again that hunting has got to be one of the goddamnedest studies of emotional dichotomy there probably ever will be. It's like love itself, one minute it's liable to be boring as hell, and the next there is so much excitement you forget there is even a world outside of this moment. Time and mass and energy all morph into one entity. Antelope hunting, especially, has all the concepts of classic and modern physics wrapped up in a package on the prairie. Out here, in September, distance never more so equals rate times time, every action has an equal and opposite reaction, and it's all relative.

"Sonofabitch," I said. "There's an antelope walking right past the truck. And it's a big-ass buck!"

Once again, there was me saying, "Get down."

There're these certain phrases that are spoken between hunting partners throughout the day. Maybe this is why it can also be such an international sport, because all you have to know how to say is:

"Get down."
"Shhhh."
"There they are."
"You missed. Shoot higher / lower / left / right."
"Good shot."
"Hand me my rifle / knife / beer / coffee / Copenhagen / rope."

And in this case I also got to say, "He's walking right to us, so let's just sit still and see how close he gets."

We had to be sticking out like a sore thumb. We had no cover, nothing, so we just sat still as the buck angled toward us. At 500 yards, with no optical enhancement, I could see he was a shooter in anyone's book, and maybe a wall hanger.

At about 200 yards I figured we'd better not wait anymore, we were just too exposed — and antelope are neither blind nor stupid. "Okay, I think you'd better

208

take a shot," I said. "Just aim right behind his shoulder and try to touch one off just like at the range."

POW!

I didn't see where the bullet hit, or if it hit, or whether it missed, but the shot was like a starting gun at an Olympic sprint. The buck was off to the races. "Lead him by about fifteen feet and keep on shooting," I said. I wouldn't be surprised if I was hollering this out loud, I was so damn excited at that point; probably more excited than Juliana was.

The buck was quartering toward us and covered the remaining distance in about five seconds; enough time for her to get off two more shots. And the last one got him! Holy shit! First time shooting at a big-game animal and it's at an antelope running full speed, and she got him! He didn't drop immediately, but I could see the impact and the wound as he sizzled by us at about fifty yards and dropped out of sight over the low ridge.

I was all kinds of stoked, but years of learning how to repress that excitement when necessary have paid off. We weren't done yet. "Shit, you got him! Good job babe! He's ours, you got him!" I was happy, but not yelling.

She immediately stood up to go get him. "We need to go get him. Let's go get him!" It was her turn to be excited.

"Huh-uh. Let's just hang for a second and calm down; and you can reload. He's hit hard. He's not going to go far."

We found him just over that low ridge, and unfortunately he wasn't dead yet. I had really hoped we'd find him stacked up so this part would be easy. But this is hunting. He was pretty much done, but still moving slowly at an angle away from us; somewhere between 75 and 100 yards. I knelt down and put the .257 crosshairs on him, but Juliana stopped me. "This is my deal," she said. "I'll finish it."

"Okay," I replied, "but you don't have to. I can do this part."

"Nope."

"Lie down and put your rifle across this rock then. And take your time, he's not going anywhere."

A crack and a thump, and it was over. The .243 will really wallop an antelope, and that's good; it didn't have to suffer very long. It hit him so hard he pretty much just disappeared into the brush.

Fifteen years ago I would have been redneck hollering. "Yeehaw! Oh yeah, you got him! Sweet shot girlie!" I'm past that now, for better or worse, so I simply put my hand gently on her back and told her that was a good shot and that now we can go get him. Now the work starts. I was trying my hardest to carefully craft these next dirty parts into as organic an experience as I could. After all, wasn't a lot of her reasoning to do this along the lines of being true to her culinary art? I was all about making an animal into a carcass, she was all about turning that carcass into some delicious wild-game dishes.

"Geeze, they're a lot smaller than I thought," she marveled. "I bet Dallas is bigger!" Our German Shepherd was indeed nearly as big as an antelope. Though I did mentally concur (their bodies always look so huge in the scope), my reaction was *Holy shit, this is a big buck!*

There, lying in the sagebrush, was an antelope buck with a set of horns bigger than any other antelope buck anyone in our family had ever killed. Fifteen years ago I would have been mildly jealous. Now I couldn't have been happier. The size of course was lost on Juliana, who had no real perspective. The first round looked like it had banged through the liver, a little back of the firebox. But it was definitely lethal, even before the kill shot she had put through the middle of his neck.

Of course we had left our packs at the truck. Of course. If you learn *one thing* from all these stories, it's that you don't ever leave your pack at the truck. Ever. At best, you're gonna have to walk all the way back down there and get it, and at worst, you could die a miserable death in the night when you have no fire, no food, and no water after you lose yourself. Thankfully, the shitty weather had passed, and all that was left was a beautiful Western sky over a pristine prairie.

The thing about antelope is that you've got to skin them right there in the field. The hair is loaded with lanolin, and if you don't remove the skin quickly, the meat will have a flavor that's way too strong. Plus, skinning helps cool the carcass off quicker, and antelope hides are nearly worthless anyway. One thing

211

I learned about doing this is that a tarp makes it much easier! So in addition to the regular field dressing procedure, we put the antelope on a small blue plastic tarp I'd brought in my pack and proceeded to skin him. I started at the belly, where I'd done the skinning to gut him out, and moved down, around, over and up. It's a pretty straightforward task, unless you're going to cape the animal for taxidermy. I did not do that in this case for two reasons: one, Juliana wasn't interested in paying for the full shoulder mount, and two, the 100-grain .243 bullet had put a sizable hole in the antelope's neck.

My wife Juliana with her first antelope

An hour later the carcass was cooling off in Birch Creek while we munched on Doritos and drank non-alcoholic beers — even fake beer tastes good after a day of hard work. Four hours after that we washed our hands in the kitchen sink and looked over a pile of packages ready for the freezer. No bonehead stunts on my part this time about hanging an animal in 50-degree temperatures for a week, wrapping the packages without first putting them in plastic wrap, and no sealing the butcher paper packages with black electrician's tape. This was another step closer to culinary art for Juliana, and it had to be done carefully.

Age has had an effect not only on my idea of what constitutes a good hunt, but also on my preferences for what I eat. I could take a whole book to discuss it (which I may just do someday), but I once weighed 330 pounds and now I weigh less than 200. In other words, I now care about what I consume, and meat is not just meat.

Arguably, the best cut of meat from wild game is the tenderloin. This is the muscle underneath (ventral to) the spine and because it's used for posture rather than for helping the animal move, it's tender. I always cut these off first and then you can make a few steaks out of them. On an antelope, they're tiny, so you might get one or two steaks if you're lucky. On an elk, they're damn near as big as a beef cow's, so you're gonna get several awesome steaks out of those, provided you didn't put a bullet through them. On the back side of the backbone (dorsal to the spine) are what most wild game butchers call the backstraps. I just call them sirloins, though I realize that's not quite the proper terminology. Whatever you call it, they're quite a bit bigger than the tenderloins, not quite as tender, but still really flavorful (think New York steak). After that you've got all kinds of awesome cuts to work at.

There're rib steaks and round steaks and roasts galore. All the rest of the "trim" you can make into hamburger, sausage, and jerky—and many people take the last little scraps and stuff them into pint jars and can them.

Now, nearly a year later, two sets of antelope horns hang on a custom plaque, which hangs on the wall of our home office. The big buck is my sweet wife's first kill, and the smaller one is my antelope, which I shot on the Saturday following the opening day. Juliana had to be back at work, so I took my mom, her husband, and my little boy with me. This second hunt was over by 9:00 in the morning, and William still talks about how the antelope "flung himself" after the flat crack of .257 split the air on a silent prairie morning not long after dawn. So now I've got Juliana and Will on board, and perhaps Sam will also warm to the sport some day.

17—November Below Heart Mountain

GEOLOGY DOESN'T EXCITE ME in ways that it might other people. I don't collect rocks, or climb rocks, but there *is* something about mountains. Mountains haunt me the way waters haunted Norman Maclean. The fact that the highest mountains have snow on them all year, even when the sun beats down on a summer afternoon in the valley, somehow adds testimony to their resistant and seemingly unchanging bearing. In our lifetimes, the mountain won't perceptibly move, but sometime, long after we're gone, that mountain won't be there anymore. This is what haunts me; this is the daunting aspect of time, the metaphorical "blink of an eye" that constitutes the moment that our lives will be juxtaposed with the life of that mountain. It just doesn't seem to make any sense.

Sometimes when circumstances seem to make no sense, though, the quick passing of my own life as it's happening makes more sense than ever. When the shit is hitting the fan, it should never be clearer to me that life is short. So really, why should you worry so much?

If you can't slow down for a second and make this statement to yourself, and live it, then you're experiencing clinical anxiety. You've got a chemical imbalance, man, and you'd better do something about it, because even the most beautiful and powerful mountain won't do anything for you. Only *you* are powerful enough to fix that. How can you be stronger than a mountain?

But mountains do have healing power, as do forests of trees, prairies of sagebrush, and elk, rifles, and backpacks. If you can combine those together somehow, at the right place and time, with the man who seems to need that medicine the most, there's a good chance he might be able to pull out of a nosedive.

How many times have I told myself to dress for the coldest possible weather? I mix up and change the words of some kid on my fire crew years ago, words about how much water to add to the freeze-dried chicken and rice packet I was preparing when we took a lunch break on a big project fire. He saw that I had put way too much water into the packet and, trying to be helpful to the boss, said to me, "You know that you can always put more water in, but you can't take the water out?" Well, duh! But then, if I'm so damn smart, why didn't I know that in the first place? So I mix those words up now and apply them to my current situation where I'm freezing my ass off up here on the mountain. Regarding clothes, I think to myself, "Why the hell didn't you bring too many clothes, instead of not enough? You can always take them off."

216

There were elk everywhere! I couldn't then and still don't believe the irony. The lead-in is that I had not yet killed a bull elk. Yep, there it is. I hadn't done it yet, and now I was looking at at least ten legal six-point bulls in full view from our vantage point, and all I cared about was that I had taken a leak a few minutes ago, and the zipper on my fucking blue jeans was frozen shut. I had had at least a gallon of coffee so far that morning, so I was having to go every few minutes. On top of that, I had been fooled by the mountain and not dressed warmly enough; down in the valley it was damn near shirt-sleeve weather. I was a frozen and pissy mess. There is plenty of comedy in hunting if it's looked at from the proper perspective, but I *wasn't* laughing. I was with my dad and his buddy, and being thirty-five years younger, I thought I ought to at least be able to withstand the cold and not bitch like a little crybaby. It was getting harder and harder by the minute.

External discomfort that goes beyond the norm will kick the ass of someone who is on shaky internal ground. The problem is that you can get yourself in a pickle, and if you're stable, it's not so bad, but if you already had issues before you even started the day, the pickle becomes a dragon that consumes all that surrounds you. Eventually I started having some serious anxiety issues. The mountain looked bigger than it should be, the trails we had ridden our four-wheelers on seemed much steeper and narrower, the temperature seemed to drop low enough to freeze hell over, and I couldn't stop shivering. My teeth were chattering. *How is this fun?* I felt like a helpless little kid again, and I was beginning to wonder just how in the fuck I was going to get off the mountain. I didn't even feel capable of walking back down, let alone negotiating an ATV full of gear down the two-track road. I used to fly in helicopters into forest fires in this wild country. I used to ride trails like this on my Honda in the middle of the night while drinking beers number 12 through 20. I used to ride green-broke horses on trails half-again as narrow and twice as steep as these, while half asleep and dreaming of being a rancher. I competed in bareback bronc riding in high school, was co-captain and middle linebacker on a state championship football team, played a little college football at that same position, and wasn't half bad as an amateur boxer. How exactly do you go from that to wanting to curl into a fetal position and repeat *There's no place like home?*

All the while my dad and his buddy kept whispering to each other. "There's a herd there." "Holy shit, look at the size of that bastard walking up the sidehill through that timber." "Couple of raghorns just below us." On and on they went.

It was like a mini version of the elk refuge outside of Jackson, Wyoming. This really was the tag and the elk hunt of a lifetime, and all I wished for was a lamp and a genie to grant me just one wish: Get me the hell out of here.

I can't even remember the balance of the morning, I just remember eventually being back at the trucks, down in the valley. It was so warm and pleasant and safe. I ate a turkey sandwich that had only dark meat (what a score) and promptly fell fast asleep in the cab of my Toyota pickup. The sun beating down through the windshield was better than any blanket. After a while we returned to the mountain to look over the elk until dark. I was shivering in my skin and even into my soul. Something was seriously the matter with me. An eight-year-old kid at Disneyland should want to be at Disneyland, and I should want to be on this hunt.

We returned to the mountain again a week later, and for every day in between, I must have taken a year off my life worrying about those goddamn four-wheeler trails. Seriously, I remember driving a 25,000-pound Type 4 fire engine up a two-track road narrower than these, on a grade so steep and with rocks so loose that the front end of that vehicle was hopping up and down like it was jumping rope. It didn't even faze me! Now I was lying in bed at night imagining all these horrific situations in which my wheeler, my gear, and I were skidding off the trail and over a cliff into Slate Basin, 100 feet below.

Enough now about mental problems, except for the one sick fact that has to be addressed, and that's that when you worry so hard and so much about something bad that might happen, the sick mind often says to itself, as a means of some kind of control: "I will not wait for bad things to happen, I will go cause them, so at least I have control over when they happen." And so now you have opened a new battle front—if not an entirely new theater of war—against yourself.

The "disease to please" for me was evidently more powerful than mental health or even my own self-preservation, because two more times I agreed to go out with my dad and his buddy to look for elk in the steep and rocky freezer that this hunting unit had become. It was almost impossible to say no. I mean, who in their right mind would turn down an offer to be taken for free on an elk hunt like this?

Right mind indeed. I was never cold again, but I kept having really wicked issues, and fought it every step of the way.

However, if there is one thing about anxiety issues that can sometimes be of benefit, it's that they make a guy hyper-aware of his situation. It's like you have super-powers when it comes to vision and spatial relationships and planning. Each time we went, I noticed that the elk we were looking at were just that; elk we were looking at. We just drove around and glassed and never made any game plans. We saw a lot of elk that way, but always at distances we couldn't reach with projectiles even if they had originated from the barrel of a howitzer. I started to make a plan for the last time I was ever going to go on this hunt. And I invited Jimmy Buffett to go with me.

It's pitch dark outside the arc of my Honda's headlights and maybe it's cold, but it isn't penetrating my layers of thermal armor this morning. Touching my skin is just a white t-shirt, but from there out, the layers get thicker and more expensive. The next layer is a long-sleeve shirt made from that old-school long-john material. On top of that is a button-up chamois shirt, then a hoodie exercise sweatshirt, then a plaid-wool jack shirt, and finally a huge Columbia parka. Covering my legs are long underwear underneath sweatpants, which are underneath wool pants. I have a $120 pair of mittens and a balaclava that would keep your face warm on Mt. Everest. Topping all that off is the best stocking cap I could find on the Cabela's website. I'm not screwing around anymore. I used to be packing a .30-06, now I'm carrying a .338 Winchester Magnum. The bullets I had originally planned on firing at an elk weighed 180 grains, now they weigh 225 grains. I'm eating the dust of my dad's and his buddy's wheelers, but not for long, and how could I not smile when I'm listening to "Cheeseburger in Paradise" through my iPod Earbuds in the pre-dawn pitch-dark somewhere on the prairie below some of the best elk-hunting country in the American West. How odd, yet how even. I just caught myself smiling, and I have a game plan.

At the first fork in the road I give a wave to the other guys as they veer left and I turn north and head directly up the face of one long and steep, steep hill. This bare hill has given me nightmares for a month. I knew I was gonna have to eventually challenge it. It's like the bully in school who taunts you and you know that it's not an "if" you'll confront him, it's a "when" and that makes it even more unnerving than if you'd just capitulate. It will take me probably thirty minutes straight of ATV grinding to reach the top of this bastard, and it's so steep that I *cannot* stop, not even one time, because if I do I'll repeat what I heard happened to another guy on this same hill, and my wheeler will do a wheelie all the way over, and all my gear and my $5000 machine and I will be back at the bottom in a wrecked and ruined mess. This is the kind of hill that I would have eaten up and swallowed ten years ago. I would've gone up it blindfolded and reading a novel at the same time, maybe while cracking beers and smoking a cigarette. Now it's a cold and dark and forbidding and evil undefined spirit that just also happens to be the main artery right into where I know goddamn well my bull elk is. I have to do it.

The thing about these Honda four-wheelers is that they're geared so you can just about putt-putt up the face of anything and never lose power. I could probably go faster, but I don't, and my iPod is now playing "Son of a Sailor" so loud through the ear buds that I can't even hear the engine. The hill is so steep that gravity is pulling me back from the handlebars and I've got to tilt my upper body forward, just as if you were riding a horse up a steep grade. And I putt and grind and putt and grind up the mountain. Anything outside the arc of the headlights is invisible and I'm going entirely on faith that when I get to the top of this sonofabitch, the little trail will just gently roll over onto flat ground. If it doesn't, I'm fucked, and fighting this thought must be what it's like to fight Mike Tyson in real life. You'd better not lose your concentration, or you're going down hard.

At the summit, the hill makes one final attempt to rattle me—in the form of really loose gravel, which makes the wheeler hop and buck a little (and causes me to nearly shit my pants), and then there's a blown-over cornice of hard snow that I have to bust through.

And then I'm there!

I take just one moment to pat myself on the back before I shut the machine down and get ready to move. Backpack, check. Rifle, check. Have gun, will travel.

I have to move quickly to the west, up the ridge, to get to that pocket of timber. It's still pretty much pitch dark, but it won't be long now until objects start to take on visual form.

Whoa! My heart races now because I just heard a cow elk bark. Sonofabitch, they're right where I knew they were going to be! I have watched this herd of elk through 10x binocs, multiple times, as they move off the flat above that pocket of timber and over the top down into the Birch Creek drainage. This time I mean to intercept them and I will finally get my chance at a bull. I know it. This herd had several bulls in it each time I saw them, thinking they were so cool moseying away. Not this time suckers, I got you!

Just as day is breaking I pop out of the west side of the pocket of timber. I watch, astonished, as the herd is just crossing over the hill and far away. The look on my face must have been the same as the look on my former boss's face when I walked into his office and he asked "How's it going?" and I simply said "I quit" and turned back around and walked out. It was priceless (other than the $70,000 a year I was forfeiting). It's the look where the eyebrows are arch, the head tilts forward, and the jaw drops open wide enough to fit a baseball into the mouth. Only now, there are big steam clouds coming out of my mouth from huffing and puffing so hard, in order to get here so fast. But, you know what, I just have to say, "So be it, Jedi."

I sling my rifle and stomp through the snow out into the wide open flats. I guess I'll just follow them over the top. I don't know what else to do. And then for some reason my focus goes from far to near. Something is there, in the corner of my eye. My first and dumbest thought is "Who put that bull elk there?"

Thirty years of experience and the innate human predator instinct all form up into an iron and tangible hand — from nothing more than foggy and blurry memories and daydreams — and the hand yanks the cord on my collected anxieties like a chain on a naked lightbulb. I have returned. It is me like I used to be.

They call it buck fever, but in this case you'd call it bull fever because there is a bull elk standing there and I'm supposed to be shaking like a leaf. But there is none of that now — I'm calm and deliberate and all business. I promised myself this morning that I was not going to miss, no matter what. I promised myself that I would get my shot today, my shot at the elusive bull elk I'd not yet connected with. I somehow knew that today was that day. I have prepared for this moment for thirty years, those years of experience all come together in this moment, and I am not going to blow it. This is the best chance I've ever had — might ever have — at taking one of these big bastards. Evidently the elk is going to cooperate as well; he's just standing there broadside, 400 yards away, watching me toss my backpack into the snow in front of me, watching me flop down prone, and watching me level my .338 Winchester Magnum at him. Every other elk I've ever encountered would have been at least in the next drainage, if not the next county, by then. Maybe there is more chance and luck to hunting than I'd previously thought. Why isn't this big boy bugging out?

I catch a last glance of Heart Mountain through the diamond ice crystals that form in the air on frigid winter mornings. There's a curl of snow blowing off the mountain as I shimmy on my elbows through the snow mattress and into shooting position. Perfect rest: rifle across the ditched backpack, my left hand settled under the forestock just in front of the scope, right hand on the pistol grip of the stock, trigger finger inside the trigger guard because now it's game time, my thumb clicking the safety into the fire position.

At this point, if I had a case of buck fever, my scope's crosshairs would be moving in figure-eight patterns around my target as I tried in vain to control my excited breathing and racing heart rate. I'd want it to be just like a practice session at the range, but it wouldn't be. The only similarity between that experience and this would be the rifle. Under the influence of buck fever, I wouldn't squeeze the trigger smoothly like I had been taught; I'd slap or pull that thing like I was trying to separate it from the rifle.

But I don't have any of that right now. My crosshairs glue immediately to that area just behind the front shoulder, which we call the "firebox" because behind it are the heart and lungs, and a quick and humane death. I squeeze the modified trigger to the crisp point of contact and CRACK! the shot is off. Then it's kind of like teeing off at the golf course: I'm not supposed to raise my head and admire my work. I'm supposed to stay focused on that target as best I can for that post-shot split-second.

On cold mornings, a rifle report gets eaten up pretty fast across an open flat, even a report from a belted magnum. It seems more like a sharp clap, but it's definitely out of place in the silence. If you make a good shot, you can often hear a subsequent slap or thud when the sound of the bullet making contact with the animal returns to you. There is no slap or thud now, at least none that I hear. In fact, after the quick crack of the rifle, everything returns to exactly as it was before. The bull is still standing, just looking at me. So on instinct, I work the bolt on my Weatherby and put round number two in the chamber. Same glued crosshairs, same steady squeeze, same rifle report. Same result. This time, though, the bull decides he's had enough and the big rack swivels to the left— and he starts galloping the hell out of there.

And now here comes the buck fever. I was wondering when I'd lose it, and at the same time, not so sad about that, because herein lies the fun! Including the shell in the chamber, a Weatherby Vanguard Series 2 rifle in .338 Winchester Magnum has four rounds. Two are now spent, and the other two immediately leave that rifle as if it were fully automatic and not a bolt action. BANGBANG. Anyone within earshot probably heard three total shots, because only the first two had any time-space between them; it would have sounded like BANG-BANG-BBANG from a distance.

And the elk crosses over the top looking perfectly healthy. The last thing I see is that rack cresting the ridge.

The ridge the bull crossed over after being shot;
he headed down into the timber on the far side.

227

There are sometimes those moments in hunting where you're like, "What just happened?" This is now. Although this is exactly what I have prepared for, it still didn't go down exactly as planned—and I like it when things go as planned. I have to fight the urge to run over to where I last saw the elk and look for its carcass or a blood trail. But this isn't a book or a movie, where I can engage the left hemisphere of my brain and skip around and do what it takes to tell a story or write a song—I can't just be crazy and creative here. I have to fire up the weaker side of my brain, the one that's responsible for logic. This is more like a story problem in math than it is a hunting tale; I have to figure out what it's asking me, define the variables, show my work, and deduce the solution.

First, I double-check my rifle situation. Empty. I fish around in my pockets and manage to find four rounds—fresh 225-grain Remington Core-Lokt Pointed Soft Point rounds. My hands are shaky trying to accomplish this otherwise simple task. Goddammit, I just want to go running over across the prairie and collect my trophy. Next, I festoon the area around me with blaze orange surveyor's tape—sure as shit I'll get over to where I thought the elk was and then get confused about where I was or where he was. With the shooting area identified like a crime scene, I can look back from over there and kind of get like an azimuth, giving me a better idea of his last location before he crested over that ridge.

But this must be my lucky day. I can already spot blood smears and specks before I even get all the way over there. My heart rate increases and the urge to run him down like I'm a wolf returns to me. Stop, get hold of yourself. This has to be more academic and less dramatic for a little while here. Think. Think carefully. I'm standing there, looking down at the blood trail in the snow, trying to define g as a function of f when movement ahead of me at about fifty yards makes me drop to my knee and bring up my rifle. Evidently the bull didn't make it all the way over the top. His position gives me only two places to shoot at: the back of his head or right up his asshole. I choose the latter because it's kind of like a bull's-eye on a paper target (maybe they should call it a "bull's-ass" instead of bull's-eye just to match the number of them on a paper target with the anatomy of a normal elk). I want this elk on the ground. Fortunately I miss; I can't imagine what a mess a shot like that would create. Now I've screwed my last chance of removing this elk from the mountain in anything resembling an easy day. At the sound of the shot he headed down into the rat's nest of thick timber on the lee side of the ridge.

He's hit hard, judging from the blood in the snow and the fact that he was already lying down within 100 yards of where he was standing when I shot. I need to calm down; he isn't going anywhere far from here. So what do I do? I charge over the ridge and down the other side. Again, this is relatable to a math problem, but I'm working at it the way an anxious high school Algebra II C+ student would work at it. Instead of following laws, theorems, and principles, I go right into trial and error.

The bull jumps up again, barely after he'd made it into the timber. BANG! And away he runs again. How the hell could I have missed?

It really is time to chill out for a minute. I even go so far as to hike back up the ridge, get on the walkie-talkie, and try to raise my dad and his buddy.

"Go ahead Ben," I hear him say. "Hey, I hit one over here, but I think I'm going to need some help." I have earlier described the yin of hunting with a partner; this is the yang — it's sure nice to have backup sometimes, especially when the backup is my old man.

Want to know really why I need help? The truth is I have two shells left, and no more. The rest of them are on my dad's wheeler. I remembered putting my leather bullet-holder pouch in one of the pockets on the camo bag attached to the rear rack of the four-wheeler. Hell, who needs more than one bullet, let alone two or four, now six or more? I'm not proud of myself for this misstep, but so be it, Jedi. I don't want to get down into that thick timber, miss two more times, and then grab the barrel of my rifle and wrap it around a tree out of frustration. I even decide to build a nice little fire to sit by, eating a granola bar while I wait for them.

My dad's buddy is with me as we descend the slope to finish the game. We haven't gone a hundred yards and the bull stands up in front of me at nearly point-blank range. POW! I can see the impact right through the center of his neck. And He. Just. Stands. There.

In fury that the game now continues into double overtime, and in amazement at the power and stamina of a bull elk, and astonished at the will this bull has to stay alive—and in my raw emotion and sadness and empathy for this beautiful animal, I yell out, "Just die, fucker!" and then I put one more right into the firebox. If that doesn't do it, this is some kind of zombie elk. He takes two or three more steps, and then he is no longer a he, he is an it—a carcass of meat on the mountain.

Dad and I with the bull from below Heart Mountain

I am sad this time. It isn't anticlimactic and vague at all. There was a very well-defined ending here, and now I'm kind of emotional about it. What's even more odd is that I'm glad I'm emotional. Too many times in my life I have shelved these emotions and they've come back to get me late in the night when I'm all alone.

231

I feel good, bad, and yeah, it was kind of ugly. But it's done. There is a beautiful 5x5 bull elk on the ground at my feet. It's not a six-point, not a 340-class monster, but it's mine. Maybe all is not fair to the elk in the game of hunting when you have high-powered rifles with crystal-clear optics and ATVs and GPS and other tools at your disposal, but I have worked for thirty years for this bull. He's mine.

18—Next Fall

ON MY SIDE OF THE STREAM the willows were almost too thick to negotiate, and although the creek was fairly wide here, it wasn't too deep; my tall Danner boots were exceptionally impermeable to water. I considered it a worthwhile endeavor, because on the far side of the stream a good-sized patch of quaking aspen began, and I always picture a big mule deer buck hanging out in the aspens. Beyond that the hunting country looked even better. I could walk a couple of hundred yards across a sagebrush flat that continued up some gentle, gullied foothills. If none of that country produced, there were always the timbered canyons above the lower draws where I could roll rocks and wait for the deer to bust out of the trees onto the steeper open sidehills.

No doubt I would connect today, but before I crossed the creek to hunt in earnest, I just sat down on a patch of grass above the willows and took in the absolute harmony and untouchable beauty of Montana's nature in October. Of course the fall colors were in full palette now, but that was just the appetizer. The full production could be experienced only if you were lucky me, and could feel the fifty-degree weather that required only a long-sleeved shirt and a sweatshirt. If you could only see the individual parts of the stream making up the more glorious whole, and in that whole you could see the very subtle workings of the distant cirrus clouds and the taller trees of the nearby aspen grove.

The stream clicked and gurgled over the geological features created by its waters. I even heard a small trout or two break the surface either upstream of me, no doubt gulping emerging caddis flies—that little splash that triggers an extra heartbeat in the chest of a trout fisherman. A small swoosh through the leaves of the trees or a moan or squeak from an old snag swaying in the slight breeze were the only other sounds.

If I could control my own aging chronological destiny, I would pause time right here and right now for at least two-sevenths of eternity, while I tried to figure out what it all meant and how it could be expressed so perfectly in one day—and felt so immediately and entirely by the human physical senses. In reality though, I was still merely a mortal human being, and a man with a mission. Or more or less a mission. I had taken time off from work and left my family at home; I'd purchased over the years untold hundreds of dollars of equipment, licenses, and tags to harvest mule deer bucks. I realized that although this moment could not last, with any luck there would be many more of these to come. And with these earthly thoughts, I quietly rolled forward, stood up, hitched my rifle and pack, and crossed the creek.

I scrambled over the gravel of the far bank and shook my feet a little, like a cat, to get most of the water off. I picked my way slowly through the nooks and crannies of twigs created by the deadfall. The leaves that had already dropped laid a yellow carpet before me and made my sneaking feet surprisingly quiet. I shifted my eyes back and forth ahead of me, sweeping the terrain to spot a deer before it spotted me. I cradled my Winchester, with its walnut stock and blue barrel, in my left arm, barrel pointed slightly back behind me, my thumb covering the bolt.

It was about 3:00 in the afternoon when I finally emerged on the north end of the aspen stand and crossed a game trail headed east into the foothills. I had a sip of ice-cold water from the tube on my camelback, then followed along the game trail. The deer and elk that used this trail had left behind plenty of tracks and scat to betray their presence, and where it crossed a wash there was a good-sized pile of fresh deer pellets.

As I got closer to the foothills, the trail kind of petered out, so I left it behind and began a gentle climb up the south side of one of the draws, eyes scanning all the time. My plan was to top out on the ridge above me by 4:30 or so, then find a place to sit where I could glass the half-dozen or so shallow draws and gulches to the north of me. Soon the deer would leave the relative safety of their bedding areas and would begin to show themselves in one of the numerous parks or in the scattered timber of the sidehills as they commenced their evening browsing.

I took two or three breaths, silent but deep, when I reached my ridgetop vantage point. The absolute stillness and the fragrance of sage made me anxious with anticipation. Something told me it was going to get exciting before too long. Making the first sweeps with my binoculars gave away no deer yet.

Movement 200 yards below me on the left caused my heart to race and my mind to go on full alert. Bringing up my binocs, I scanned the saddle below and positively identified the large gray body of a lone mule deer buck. He was at least a 3-point, probably a 4-point, and that was good enough for me. I sat and watched him, and the field around him, for about a minute. Deciding that he had no bigger friends coming to join him, I prepared for the shot.

Right then I was experiencing one of the many reasons I could never quit hunting altogether — it's the rush that accompanies this ultimate moment. Very slowly I edged over to the boulder next to me and leveled my rifle across it, resting on a blaze-orange sweatshirt spread over the rock's surface. The buck stood broadside to me, facing uphill. I picked him up in my crosshairs and flicked off the safety with my right thumb. My right index finger found the trigger, and I adjusted the crosshairs so they were resting on the area directly behind his shoulder. Trying to calm my beating heart, I gradually increased pressure on the trigger until it broke. Then came the crack and thud of a well-placed shot.

The buck leapt forward and then reversed direction, headed headlong back downhill toward a small group of trees. I quickly worked the bolt to eject the spent cartridge and replace it with a new one, but it was unnecessary. The buck stumbled and collapsed into the brush. I blew out a sigh of air and found myself shaking a little. It was absolutely still and silent again, just like that.

The next moments were spent doing what I had done many times before, remaining silent and still, trying to collect myself. I watched the buck through my binocs, making sure he was not going to get up and go anywhere. I did this for about ten minutes, until I judged myself ready to make a move.

That first move was to put a streamer of orange tape on a sapling to mark my spot, in case I got disoriented when I was down the hill. The next step was to unchamber the .30-06 cartridge, sip some more water, and began to work my way across the draw and down toward the deer.

He was easy to find, his antlers the first thing I spotted. A beautiful and symmetric 4x4, about twenty-four inches wide. I could ask for no better. I knelt down and patted the deer between his ears. Looking around me, I took in the moment provided by nature. It was now approaching 6:00 and would be getting dark soon, so I was not able to do much reflecting. I repositioned the buck and took out my field-dressing tools. Now the work begins.

Acknowledgments

Disagreements among my dad and my brother Tom and me can sometimes lead to the point where it seems the only way to solve the difference is a fistfight. While this has happened only a few times, and hasn't happened for at least fifteen years now, I have come to the realization that the only people I have ever been in fights with are those I care about. I am aware there isn't any outward logic to this, but on a deeper plane, I would never exert much effort toward someone I don't like, and sometimes that effort involves anger. It's the peaks and valleys thing, or maybe better understood as when there is never any rain, there's a desert below. There is no desert of emotions with my dad and my brother and me, and without them, I wouldn't have much of a hunting story, so my first thank-you has to be to them—and I mean it with all my heart. And fellas, if you don't like that, we can always go outside and settle it!

My wife is my best friend, and she is always there encouraging me to make new stories and write them down so we can always remember these crazy and sometimes rugged days that all too soon turn into the good old days. I am eternally thankful to her for her patience and quiet perseverance and the calmness she adds to my life.

I also have the utmost gratitude and respect for my editor Kelly Andersson. She works with some of the best and most experienced writers there are, yet she still takes the time to help a novice author like me turn a ratty manuscript into something fun to read. If boxing and fighting would be metaphors for writing and life, you definitely want Kelly in your corner of the ring, and she will always have your back out there in the streets of life. Thank so much and so always Kelly!

About the Author

BEN WALTERS is a reformed party animal, former wildland firefighter, and former schoolteacher who lives in Idaho Falls, Idaho with his awesome and loving wife and children. After bunches of years, bunches of jobs, tons of good times, and a couple of college degrees, he realized it was time to settle down and start putting some of these experiences to paper before the words of his youth slipped away.

His first book, FIRE CREW, was called "an extraordinary epic, spirited and engaging and educational." In that book he journeys from an awkward and raw sense of wildland firefighting to a firm purpose of becoming the very best version of a wildland firefighter.

www.ingramcontent.com/pod-product-compliance
Lightning Source LLC
Chambersburg PA
CBHW072123270326
41931CB00010B/1646